First Comes the Wind

Margaret Jensen

Gordon
College

Reprinted with author's permission by Gordon College Printing Services, 2003.

Originally published by
HERE'S LIFE PUBLISHERS, INC.
P.O. Box 1576
San Bernardino, CA 92402

Library of Congress Cataloging-in-Publication Data
Jensen, Margaret T. (Margaret Tweten), 1916—
    First comes the wind.
    I. Title.
PS3560.E593F5 1986   813'.54   86-9847

Acknowledgements

Special thanks to Gordon College and Gordon College Printing Services.

Contents

Acknowledgments

A special thanks, not only to my immediate family for their love and support, but also to my extended family, Myrtlegrove Presbyterian Church and our beloved pastor emeritus, Horace Hilton.

And a special thanks to the other part of my extended family, the staff of Here's Life: Les Stobbe, Dan Benson, Jean Bryant, John Crone, JoAnne Gingles, Wayne Hastings, Margie Hill, Don Reiter, Terry Smith, Doug Weaver, and all the staff, for their love and support and patience.

And another special thanks to Evelyn Bence and to a new friend, Doris Fell who made me look good.

one

The Storm

*M*y sweat-soaked shirt clung to me as I stacked the last tree stub on the woodpile. I sank the ax into the chopping block behind my Grandmother Lundstrom's sturdy two-story home that overlooked Wrightsville Beach. That old sun-bleached house had weathered three generations of Lundstroms and more than one hurricane since my grandfather, Big Lund, the old man of the sound, had built it for his bride sixty years ago.

Brushing woodchips from my hands, I stomped in the back door, grabbed a glass of iced tea and headed for the dining room. I stopped short in the doorway and studied my eighty-year-old grandmother. She sat at the large oak table, her gnarled hands on a magnifying glass, her open Bible inches from her fingers. She was frail now, her salt and peppery hair long ago lost to a snowy white. Her chin quivered slightly. Or was she praying for me as she had for my father?

"Good morning, Noragram," I said, quickly walking over and planting a kiss on her wrinkled brow.

She looked up, her faded blue eyes brightening. Her strength was in her gaze, penetrating, confident. "Well, young man, I wondered how long it would take you to speak up."

For an instant, I shrank from twenty-seven to a boyish ten. "I didn't want to disturb you," I apologized. "You seemed deep in thought."

"This is my reflecting table," she answered softly. "I do all my reminiscing from here." She ran her wrinkled, workworn hand across the table top, caressing it, polishing it as she had done over the years.

"Have you decided to move into the city with Wilma Newton like I suggested — get away from this forsaken area?" I asked guardedly.

"You think this house is getting out of hand, too much for me?"

"No," I managed. "I just worry about you alone out here on the beach. Especially during hurricane season."

"But I've got me some neighbors. Good ones." She smiled. "I keep hoping you'll be staying on yourself, Lundy — coming home for good."

I shifted restlessly. "Arizona's my home now. My work — my business."

"So you're still thinking about taking over Thornton Enterprises?" Her tone was accusing.

"My father made a good living there." I met her gaze defiantly. "Besides, there's nothing to hold me here in Wrightsville."

Noragram nodded toward the ocean. Rebecca Cranston was sauntering along the isolated beach, her long, flowing hair as ivory-colored as the sand, her innocent face lifted to the wind.

"Rebecca's reason enough," Grams answered.

"I know." I hesitated, not wanting to wear my feelings on my sleeve. "But I've tried to win her. Even proposed. She doesn't want me, Grams. She'll only settle for a godly man." I sat down across from my grandmother, turning the glass of iced tea in my hand.

"You've begun, though, haven't you, Lundy? You've sprouted a seed — met Jesus. You don't grow up to maturity overnight."

Grams was right. I'd begun the journey months ago but in many ways I was still floundering. "You're avoiding my question, Noragram," I said.

"Question?" she repeated.

"Yeah. The one that says let's close up the place and move you into town."

"Never," she said emphatically, a crisp edge to her voice. Her sweeping gesture included the beach, the ocean. "This is my land."

"But I worry about you. The hurricane season will be here before you know it."

She chuckled, laugh lines turning her ancient face merry. "The Lundstroms are good stock. They've weathered many a storm, Lundy."

"But you've had some close calls too," I argued. "You're no match for the hurricanes."

"God is," she said flatly. She reached across the oval table and rested her fragile, tissue-thin hand on mine. "It's been the Lundstrom's land for generations. It's your land, too, Lund Lundstrom, and it was your father's before you."

I drew my hand away. "My dad's land?" I scoffed. "If it was his land, why did he leave it? Why did he run out?"

"He came back," she said softly. "My son came back."

"Sure. In a box," I retorted. I glared out the dining room window toward the Atlantic. Lovely Rebecca Cranston stood at the shoreline, the waves rippling over her bare feet. The ocean was peaceful today, calm like Noragram. But it could be ferocious, violent — its fury smashing everything in its path, lashing out as my father had lashed out at life. As I remembered those days long past, the ocean and my father's fury blended as one, beating fiercely in my own breast.

"Grams, I'm still worried about you," I told her defensively. "You might not have your radio or TV on — you might not hear the hurricane warnings."

Noragram patted her hearing aid and chuckled again. "I might not hear the warnings, Lundy. But I'll know if a storm is brewing." She thumped her chest, then pointed to *the ocean. "I knew back in 1954 before Hurricane Hazel hit the coast. It's just like the stirrings in life, Lundy. Before every storm, first comes the wind."*

* * *

On that frightening day in October, 1954, the sea rose and churned with a vengeance, sending angry waves to tear at the man-made dunes on Wrightsville Beach. Screaming winds whipped at the pier's foundations. Boats, torn from their moorings, bobbed futilely, then disappeared beneath the monstrous waves. The waves slapped at brand new homes and cupped up the North Carolina beach front in a gigantic hand that swept lawns and pilings from shorefront cottages out to sea.

Leonora Lundstrom, a small woman with hazel eyes and short-cropped brown hair, braced herself against the wind as she wrapped her gray cape around her thin shoulders. Below the rim of the berm she watched the ocean grasp relentlessly for the coastline. Behind her she could hear the radio warnings urging the beach residents to evacuate before Hurricane Hazel could take its deadly toll in lives and property.

But had the warnings come soon enough? At first there were advisory reports. The weather forecaster, stating, "Rain and cooler tonight." "Hurricane Hazel dawdling at sea." For hours it had been cloudy, misty at the beach, the sun breaking through briefly — mocking, daring the storm to hit.

Then more forecasts. The storm, traveling with the trade winds, was cutting northeastward. Torrential rains were hitting south of Wilmington. Endless reports came in throughout the day. Reluctantly, knowingly, Big Lund and their son Nelson boarded up the windows, carried special family mementoes and Nora's favorite chair upstairs. They had secured the cupboard doors and checked their battery-powered radio as the weather forecaster urged vigilance.

Leonora — Nora — had quietly wrapped her favorite dishes and pictures in blankets and towels and pulled the lamp cords from the wall plugs. As the barometer fell, Nelson carried the suitcases and metal box of valuables to the truck.

The rising east wind stirred up the surf and rattled the windows of the Lundstrom's home, then darkness came as the final board was nailed in place. *This wasn't an ordinary house,* Nora thought, *but one hammered out of love.* The house had stood against the storms for years — ever since Big Lund built it for her. She ran her fingers along its casings. Would it stand against Hurricane Hazel?

"Come, Nora-girl," Lund Lundstrom said as he slipped up behind her and encircled her with his protecting arm. She leaned against his rock-hard chest and sensed his strength — a big man, a towhead with distinctive Norwegian features and powerful shoulders.

For a moment they stood in the doorway staring at the raging Atlantic together. The churning, foaming surf was wild, fascinating. Leonora could no longer distinguish the long strand of beach that stretched along the shoreline. Storm gales and waves lashed over the sand dunes, splashing against the rooftops of the beach-front cottages. "Big Lund, man's genius is no match for the fury of Lady Ocean's scorn."

The roar of the seas answered the cries of the wind. "Come," Lund urged gently. "We must hurry. We've boarded up everything — secured the house and shop the best we can."

The wind whipped against them as they crossed the porch. Lund held her hand as they struggled down the steps to the truck.

Their son Nelson, a blond with a smattering of freckles and finely carved features like his dad, waited in the driver's seat, sullen and anxious. His golden-haired German Shepherd, King, huddled in the back of the truck, growling deeply at the howling wind.

Lund took a final glance at the ocean, then helped Nora into the truck. As he did so, her words seemed to be carried on the wind. "The sun will shine tomorrow, Lund. We've lived through many battles with the ocean but she always wins. I knew a storm was coming."

"Your trees told you?" Nelson asked, his face unsmiling.

"My pine trees whisper secrets, Nels. Later the sun will shine again. But first comes the wind."

As Nelson eased the car out of the driveway, Nora stole one final glance at the house — snapping a mental picture that might have to last a lifetime.

The rains hit with blinding fury as they drove toward Wilmington. Nelson crouched against the steering wheel, squinting, trying to keep the truck on a road covered with water. The engine was sputtering. They passed other cars stalled at the roadside.

"Stop, Nels," Nora begged.

"Can't, Mom," he answered, his firm jaw set. "We can't risk stalling ourselves. We'll send help back."

"It's good that the summer season has ended," Lund said reflectively. "Or there would be others trapped — "

"Man's no match for the sea, Dad. They're fools flocking here in the summer — coming for the weekends all winter long."

"Fools, son?" Lund challenged. "Where can you find sun and surf and life more challenging?"

Nels' shoulders tensed. "Or life more devastating? I'd like to try some dry land for a change. How do you stand it, year after year, running a wave's length ahead of the storm? Going back and cleaning up — starting over again?"

They rode in silence, Nora squeezed in the front seat between her two men. Storms always did this to Nels. He hated running — hated nature forcing him from his home. She had warned Big Lund, *"Nels won't always stay here. He's restless."*

Lund hadn't seen it. "But he promised, Nora-girl. Ever since he was a boy, we've been planning to build houses together. Father and son. Nels has got a knack for it."

But it wasn't building with his dad that slowed the restlessness. Nora knew it was the Newton girl — lovely Melissa.

Nels slowed as he spotted a lone figure in bright yellow rain togs waving a stop sign. Nels rolled down the window. "What's up?" he called.

Rain blew through the open window, chilling them. King snarled.

The man wiped the rain from his face. "Go carefully. The bridge is damaged. It might wash out any minute."

"Thanks," Nels answered, tight-lipped. "But my girl's on the other side of that bridge. No bridge — no storm — is keeping me from Melissa."

The man shrugged. "It's best not to try it. The river's raging."

Nels gently put his foot to the gas pedal and inched along cautiously, past other vehicles that had heeded the warning.

"Nels, are you sure, son?" Lund asked.

Nelson didn't answer. The car crept along. "One of the railings is out," he announced peering through the rain-swept windshield.

The bridge railing dangled precariously on their right as Nels coaxed the still-sputtering old vehicle along. The bridge creaked and swayed beneath their weight. Rivulets of the swollen river washed across the bride.

Nora gripped Big Lund's hand, praying. Out loud, she whispered, "Jesus, help us."

She felt Big Lund's hand enfolding her own, heard his deep voice uttering prayers of his own.

Behind them, beside them, Hurricane Hazel was riding on the wind, carrying its destructive, explosive force with it.

two

Melissa

As he neared town, Nelson's spirit quickened. He would be seeing his fiancee, Melissa Newton, in a few moments. He gripped the steering wheel, holding the truck to the road, and felt good inside. There was nothing he liked better than being with Melissa. They had grown up together, but as she had reached womanhood, Nels suddenly discovered her and fell in love with her.

Even now, he could see her lovely beauty — the soft brown hair that framed her delicate features, the wide innocent brown eyes that studied him when he proposed. The tiny, upturned nose that sun-burned in the summer. The lips that caressed him. Her lilting voice, saying, "Yes, I'll marry you."

The windshield wipers squealed across the window pane giving him fleeting glimpses of familiar streets. Not far now. Nels knew that Melissa would have the candles, kerosene lanterns and heaters out of the storage bin. By the time they got there, she would have the water jugs filled and water pouring into the bathtubs. If the electric lines went down in the storm, there would be no well water. Melissa was quick and efficient like her mother. Nels liked that about her.

Her brother Chad and her dad, Mike Newton — a good man, a good friend — would have boarded up the windows and secured the machinery in the cabinet shop behind the garage. Melissa's mother, Wilma Newton, a practical woman, planned well for emergencies. At the first storm warning, she would have made her rounds to check on supplies for her elderly neighbors. Then, before her family could protest, Wilma would be in the old Ford heading for the long line at the grocery store, buying up supplies to last them through the storm.

When Nels drove up to the house, the Newtons were still carrying in the groceries, racing against the threatening rain and wind before it could sweep them off their feet. Nels honked as he swung into the driveway. When they spotted the truck, the Newtons shouted for joy. Nels swung down from the van, grabbed Melissa in his arms and crushed her against his wet jacket. She blushed and nestled against him. "I was so frightened," she whispered. "I was afraid you wouldn't get here."

Nels threw back his head and laughed — laughed for the first time since leaving the beach. "No storm — nothing — could keep me from reaching you."

King jumped from the truck, his barks mingling with the frenzied yapping of the neighborhood dogs. The Newtons' greeting was no less enthusiastic. Everyone talked at the same time as they carried supplies and suitcases into the garage apartment reserved for the Lundstroms.

After slipping into warm, dry clothes, the Lundstroms made their way to the kitchen. A kettle of soup simmered on the stove. If the power went out, it could be kept hot on the kerosene burner. Wilma and Melissa were still putting away the groceries.

"The lines in the store were endless," Wilma panted. "I thought I'd never make it back home. Trees were bending over the road and a steady stream of cars drove in from the beach. I kept my car radio on. The announcer kept urging people along the shoreline to evacuate so I knew you folks would be coming. Didn't I tell you that, Melissa?" Nels looked at Melissa and winked. She grinned shyly.

As the winds pounded the house, Mike Newton turned to Nels's dad and said, "Big Lund, you surely did know what you were doing when you bought this land years ago and built this sturdy house for us. And not only the house but the shop for us to work from." Mike sipped his coffee. "You just don't stay in your apartment often enough. Guess it takes a storm to bring you in. But it's good to have you here now, safe and sound."

"Thanks Mike." Lund glanced at Nels. "It is good to be over that bridge. I was certain we'd go down with it. The water is rising too high for safety. The storm looks like a bad one this time."

"Hey, Dad," Nels said. "I told you nothing would keep me from Melissa."

Laughter and old memories filled the kitchen as Big Lund and Mike recalled years of building houses together, fishing trips, and oyster roasts on the Sound. While the men exchanged their views on the storm, Nelson drew Melissa toward the fireplace. Tenderly he took her in his arms while she murmured against his shoulder, "Oh, Nels, I was so afraid something would happen to you, but here you are — safe."

He tipped her chin toward him. "Forget Hurricane Hazel. I'll protect you always. In a few months you will belong to me forever. I love you, Melissa Newton."

"And I love you, Nelson Lund Lundstrom!"

Leonora and Wilma rattled dishes and exchanged their views on new recipes, the church, and the schools. One peek in the oven revealed the corn bread was brown so Wilma called the men for supper, interrupting their discussion of sports and politics.

"It's warmer in here," Wilma announced as everyone took their place around the big round table in the kitchen. "Power could go out any minute."

With hands joined together, Mike Newton prayed:

Bless this house, O Lord we pray
Keep it safe by night and day
Bless this food, we offer thanks
For home and friends."

A chorus of "Amens" blended with the whistling wind, demanding an entrance.

Laughter and memories continued as soup and corn bread made the rounds, followed by apple pie and coffee. Big Lund and Mike recounted years of working together and sharing numerous fishing trips. Leonora and Wilma told stories about the children. "Do you remember," Nora chuckled, "When Chad and Nels were young boys, how they begged us to keep Melissa from following them around?"

Wilma nodded. "And when she grew older, the boys reluctantly took her on fishing trips and even taught her to water ski on the Sound."

Everyone laughed when Nels spoke up. "Since Melissa insisted on those fishing trips, I decided to marry her so she could bait my hooks."

"Well, start looking for someone for me, Nels," Chad said, reaching for another piece of apple pie. "I still have to bait my own hooks."

"Let's get the dishes done before the power goes off." Wilma's warning brought action — and not too soon.

Just as they finished, the crash of the storm hit the house, suddenly plunging it into darkness. Mike felt his way through the darkened room to the battery radio.

Everyone drew close to the warmth of the fire and to each other as a quiet awe descended over the household, each person lost in a niggling fear. Big Lund expressed it for all of them. "I keep thinking about the beach, wondering if it's safe against the pounding ocean."

"Or if the house is still standing?" Nora asked.

Quietly Melissa took down the family Bible and turned to Psalm 91. In the flickering lamp light, she read:

He that dwells in the secret place of the most high
Shall abide under the shadow of the Almighty
I will say of the Lord

He is my refuge and my fortress,
My God, in Him will I trust . . .
Thou shalt not be afraid for the terror by night . . .
He shall give His angels charge over thee
To keep thee in all thy ways."[1]

Quietly Big Lund added, "Faith is endangered by security; but faith is secured in danger."

Melissa glanced up at Nels. "No matter what the future holds, darling, I want our faith to be secured always."

Nels shifted. "You bet," he answered uneasily.

As the evening progressed, the hurricane, like a roaring freight train, screamed over the sound and far into the city and county. Trees crashed down on streets and buildings. Rivers rose, flooding streets and homes. Chimneys blew off roofs. A church steeple tumbled. Hundred-mile-an-hour winds churned the ocean. Waves washed over the beach, leveling houses and sweeping boats, homes and bridges out to sea. Sea water bubbled through concrete, flooding basements. The winds shifted. Electric wires short-cicuited. The sky blackened.

All through the night, the men took turns standing watch. Waiting. Hoping. Praying for the storm to end.

"The sun will shine tomorrow," Nels's mom had said and so it did. A few days after the rains died down, the Lundstroms returned to their home. The surf-battered house was still standing mute against the stillness. Debris littered the beach. The winter's wood pile had washed out to sea. Boats were smashed against the dock. Cans of Nora's food cluttered the floor and one of her favorite lamps lay smashed in the corner.

But Nora seemed at peace. She bustled around her kitchen putting the coffee pot on. The storm had passed and this morning the pines whispered that a truce had been made between land and sea. At least that is how Nora explained the morning calm.

Big Lund and Nels spent the day running chain saws, cutting up debris and clearing the road in front of the house. Finally Big Lund paused, cocking his head thoughtfully. "Son, some of these trees bent with the wind, yet these giant oaks crashed helplessly in the gale." He walked a few

22

feet to another tree. "Look over here, Nels. See the tree that you and Melissa used to climb? I never thought any storm could topple that one — with its limbs so big a man could walk on them."

Nels gazed at the ragged split edge of the trunk. "Dad, look at the rot in the heart of this tree trunk."

Big Lund studied it for a moment. "No wonder it fell in the storm. There was no way to know that its roots were bad until the storm brought it down. Lands, son, I feel bad about this old oak — it's like the passing of an old friend."

Nels shrugged. "It's just a tree, Dad."

"No, son. Not really. It's like the preacher said, 'Who can know the heart of man? Who can know the hidden rot of a mighty oak.'"

Nels frowned. "Dad, I get the feeling you're not just talking about that tree."

Big Lund shook off his sadness and slipped his arm around Nelson. "Oak trees are a special part of the land I love — the land you love."

"Yeah, Dad."

Big Lund strolled across the road to the empty lot. Nels followed.

"How would you like this lot for your house, Nels — a house for you and Melissa? Grand view of the ocean. We could build together in our spare time. Right now we have to do a lot of repair work from the storm, but with Chad and Mike we could probably get your house done. Chad can do the cabinet work near town, and we could get the pilings and footings started. Nothing like building a sure foundation."

Standing on the cleared lot, overlooking the ocean, Nels placed an affectionate arm around his father. There was no way he could tell his dad that he wanted to leave the land. "Beautiful, Dad, beautiful! What a place for a house for Melissa!" Nels hoped he sounded honest, sincere. Through misty eyes he added, "Thanks, Dad, thanks for everything. There's nothing I'd rather do than work with you, building and designing for the future."

"Quite a son I have — quite a boy! While others goofed off in high school you and Chad worked with your fathers in the shops — made money for your first car and then college. Maybe I don't say it enough, but I'm mighty proud of you, Son. Yes sir, mighty proud."

Nora interrupted with a call for lunch, and the conversation turned to wedding plans in June, after Melissa's graduation from Wilmington College.

Cheerfully Nora went about the task of restoring order and cleanliness to her house and yard, wiping away the mildew and carrying out the debris. While bedding and rugs aired on the line, Nels peeked over Nora's shoulder as she made notes about the festivities of Christmas, the Women's Circle meeting at her home, a shower for Melissa's graduation and reminder to Big Lund about the floats for the Azalea Festival.

She looked up at Nelson. "I'm worried about the azaleas this year — the storm was so bad and such a cold winter predicted."

"Are you worried about the wedding, Mom?" he asked.

Nora smiled happily. "Melissa is like the daughter I never had. I'm pleased, Nelson — you're such a good son. You love your home and your family like few sons I know. I know you'll love Melissa always."

His mother had been right. The days blended into weeks and the joys of Christmas blended into the promise of spring. The wet, cold spring marred the local Azalea Festival. Big Lund had managed to complete the floats, but the rain and sleet kept the flowers and people under cover. High winds blew over New Hanover Airport. But finally, soft breezes blew the warmth and sunshine into June — Melissa's graduation and the wedding.

three

The Wedding

A glory shone in the face of their beloved minister, his white hair hung low on his forehead. His voice boomed in the June stillness. "Dearly beloved, we are gathered together in the presence of God and this assembly to witness the joining together in holy wedlock of Melissa Wilma Newton and Nelson Lund Lundstrom."

Wilma Newton felt tears of joy welling up in her heart as she gazed tenderly at her daughter. *How beautiful she looks in the silky wedding dress she made.* Wilma could almost see Melissa's big brown eyes squinting to thread the needle of the sewing machine that Mike bought her for high school graduation.

It was like yesterday. "Oh, I can make my own clothes for college," Melissa had squealed with delight. With an impulsive hug for her father, she added, "And someday I'll make my own wedding dress."

Wilma remembered Mike's soft answer as he held his daughter closer, "My little girl is growing up too fast."

25

A lump came into Wilma's throat as she recalled her yesterdays — teaching Melissa to sew, to bake bread, to keep a well-ordered home. "I'd rather go fishing with the boys, Mother," Melissa had insisted. Wilma smiled to herself. Fish she did! Boating, water sports — and taught well by the boys, but Wilma also knew that she had taught her daughter well.

How small Melissa looked standing beside Nelson and *How handsome my Mike looks* she mused. *Like a football player poured into a tuxedo — or maybe like a teddy bear in a starched shirt.*

The voice of the minister continued, "The most important decision in life is to know God personally, through His Son, Jesus Christ. For Jesus is the Way, the Truth, and the Life. Then the second most important step in life is the union of two people in marriage, for the home is the foundation of society.

"Love will make the ordinary beautiful. The caterpillar becomes a butterfly, and love paints over the drabness of winter with the pastel colors of spring. Love awakens the song of birds and keeps the embers burning. Melissa, Nelson — don't allow the flame of love to go out, for it is not easy to rekindle love."

Across the aisle from Wilma, Nora sat quietly remembering the day, thirty years ago, when she and Big Lund had heard the same words from this gentle man of God. *Even now,* she thought, *How handsome my Lund looks, standing like a big oak in a forest — all six-and-one-half feet tall.* Big Lund, a true son of Norway, his father had called him. The name Big Lund had stayed. But now, for the first time, Nora noticed streaks of gray in his blond hair.

Nels, looking much like his father, stood tall and proud, his love for Melissa shining in his deep blue eyes. How Nora loved her men! She loved them all: Chad, the bridesmaids — all grown up together. These wonderful people of the community who filled the church with joy and best wishes. The music, flowers, and candles blended with the warmth of love.

The minister's steady voice continued: "Love is like a lighted lamp. A man without love is like a lamp without a flame. Tend the flame well, Nelson Lundstrom. A virtuous woman's price is above rubies. The heart of her husband trusts in her and she will look well to the ways of her household. Her children will rise up and call her blessed. Nelson, love Melissa as Christ loves you. God does not impose His will, but draws you by His love. Do not impose your will, but draw together as a team, with love."

Nelson could not take his eyes from Melissa.

"Melissa, honor, obedience and submission aren't words to be shunned, but rather to be embraced in the light of God's will through His Word. As two becoming one, you submit to, honor, and obey God. To know God is to love God. To know each other, as you have known each other from childhood, is also to love, trust and respect each other.

"When one's heart is set to love, the fruit of love is manifested in committed obedience to God's laws and commitment to each other. Joy and peace follow. Love stands the test of time, for love is eternal."

As Melissa and Nels knelt to receive communion, the evening sun filtered through the stained-glass windows, casting a soft golden hue over the wedding. The minister's joyous introduction, "Mr. and Mrs. Nelson Lund Lundstrom," sent the music bursting through the windows, over the water, across the waves of a new tomorrow.

The fellowship hall was filled with tables loaded with Wilma's and Nora's special delicacies. For the next few hours bridesmaids fluttered like butterflies, and the men discussed politics and fishing.

Nora watched Miss Lottie, the beloved grandmother of the sound, limping toward her. "I'll tell you one thing, Nora," she sputtered. "Dr. Parks sure can tie a good knot. Even my Jake stayed awake — terrible how he sleeps in church. Never been a wedding like this one in the whole county." She shook her snowy head. "These young folks — just babies — short time ago, and now look at them, fixing to get married. Lord, have mercy! Nora, where do the years go? Come September, Jake and me been married sixty years. Heard tell the younguns plan a big to-do — ha! Think I don't know. One thing sure, I have my dress — this one.

Wilma and Melissa bought the fancy material and made it for me."

"You look right pretty, Miss Lottie," Nora assured her.

"You look good, too, Nora, mighty fetching in that blue. And Wilma, usually so plain looking, made folks sit up and take notice, walking in like a fine city lady, on the arm of that good-looking Chad. Black hair pulled back, and that soft pink lace. Mike looked so proud, thought he'd bust a button off that fancy shirt."

"We're all proud, Miss Lottie."

"Never saw so many folks since Captain Bill's funeral . . . . Never will forget the choir singing, 'I'll fly away.'"

Nora interrupted the happy chatter again. "Miss Lottie, looks like the children are getting ready to fly away, so here is your bag of rice. We had better see them off to the mountains."

"We be mighty proud of you," Miss Lottie waved to the bride and groom "and will be missing you."

Then they were off! Rattling tin cans and dragging a "Just Married" sign, they disappeared around the bend of the road as Nora watched wistfully.

Miss Lottie saw the look in her eye. "When all the kin folks leave tomorrow, Nora, why don't you and Big Lund come set a spell on my porch? Been a long time since my porch washed away in the Big Storm. Big Lund built me a new one, so you all come, pinto beans and cornbread will taste mighty good after all this fancy eating. We be missing you."

Big Lund cut in on the conversation. "I heard that, Miss Lottie, and Nora and I will be happy to sit on your new porch." Miss Lottie stomped down the road toward home, singing, "I'll fly away," while Jake ambled slowly beside her.

It wasn't long before the whole crowd had scattered and Big Lund put a loving arm on Nora's shoulder. "Come, Nora-Girl. Let's go home. There's a summer wind coming in off the ocean."

four

Melissa's House

The call of the seagulls accompanied the ringing of the hammers where Big Lund and Mike were putting finishing touches on the house for the bride and groom. As they worked, Nora tended her garden at the Big House and King chased squirrels up a tree. But the sound of Chad Newton's truck coming down the road brought everyone's work to a stop.

Nora wiped her hands on her apron, put aside her gardening tools and called across to the men, "I'll go in and put the coffee on."

As Chad stepped from the truck, he looked at Mike and said, "I finished the kitchen cabinets, Dad. That means we can get them in today."

"And done before the young folks get back from their honeymoon," Mike added.

As he looked around inspecting the progress, Chad whistled. "Whew," he said. "I never expected to see so much done. You and Big Lund have made great strides — especially with all the rebuilding that's gone on since the storm. And

29

in spite of that cold, wet spring, it looks like we're really catching up."

Nora's call for a coffee break brought Big Lund, Mike and Chad to the porch. They sighed with pleasure when they saw Nora's cinnamon rolls and the coffee pot.

"We miss Melissa," said Mike, but we know she's in good hands. Wilma has the apartment all ready for them and the refrigerator full. It's so convenient for them to have your apartment until the house is ready."

"Can't imagine life without the children close by." Big Lund's gaze went out over the ocean.

Mike interrupted. "Nothing in the world makes a man more proud than to have his son work with him. We are blessed, Big Lund. Yes sir, we are blessed."

"Well, one thing for sure," Nora said, "Wilma and I will enjoy Melissa together. Seems that's how folks used to do, live and work together. Maybe I'm old-fashioned, but I like it. Everyone has the right to his own life, to use the talent God gave him, but it also seems good to blend that talent together — as families and a community. When trouble comes we share the grief and when there is joy, we all rejoice together."

As if she were talking to herself, she kept on going, "Now I ask you, what do the big cities have that we don't have? We have the music of the ocean and the seagulls; the original of sunsets and sunrise. When our fishing boats come home in the evening or early morning, the children and neighbors run to see the catch. What stories they get from the old fishermen! We can sit on our porch and watch the young people skim over the water, better than a water show in Florida — and cheaper, too! Our gardens and fishing poles fill our freezers for winter; and hunting brings a deer or two."

"The bathing beauties on the beach aren't too bad either," Chad added, with his usual boyish grin.

Mike reached for another cinnamon roll. "Man, we haven't had time to fish lately — too much work, Big Lund. We need a good fishing trip."

Finally a "back to work" order made the hammers ring again across the waves, the seagulls screaming through the sky above them.

When the days of honeymooning came to a close, Melissa returned to Wilmington College, this time to work in the office. Nels went back to finishing Melissa's house. The days flowed into weeks and the house grew from a shell to a bridal castle; as they were working late in the fall one Saturday, Nels asked, "Do you really think we can be in our house for Christmas?"

"Only if we are invited for Christmas dinner," Mike joked.

"Wait a minute," Nora interrupted when she heard Mike. "No plans for Christmas Eve. You know I always have Christmas Eve in the Big House."

With a mocking bow, Big Lund answered gravely, "Indeed, we would never dare defy Norwegian tradition, Mrs. Lundstrom. Christmas Eve in the Big House it shall be!"

"We can still have dinner Christmas Day in Melissa and Nels's house," Mike answered.

Nels exploded with excitement and jumped down from his ladder to hug all three of his co-workers at once — his dad, Mike and Chad. With a whoop of joy he yelled, "You are formally invited to Christmas dinner at the home of Mr. and Mrs. Nelson Lundstrom."

"Might be a good idea to check with Melissa," Nora laughed.

"We better plan New Year's Day at our house, or we'll have Wilma to contend with," Mike grinned at Nora.

"I think the next stop is right here for lunch." Nora's practical suggestion brought the hammers and conversation to a close and the four men obediently washed up for lunch. As they sat down to the table, Melissa arrived, her car filled with decorator books and paint charts.

After they ate, Nora sent the men back to work so she and Melissa could spend the afternoon looking at wallpaper and paint charts. Wilma was coming with supper for everyone. Country ham, green beans, sweet potatoes and Wilma's famous biscuits. Melissa had baked a fresh coconut cake, kept hidden from the men. Nora had the ice cream freezer ready to crank strawberry ice cream.

Chain saws echoed over the sound as the men felled trees, cut the wood and stacked their winter fuel. The hammers sounded out across the water, and the sun seemed reluctant to close another day.

It was late when Melissa and Nels left for their apartment in town. After they left, Wilma and Nora washed the dishes and made plans for the holidays. "Can't plan too early," Wilma suggested.

With their feet propped up on the porch rail the men rocked slowly. "If the weather holds, the house could be ready by Thanksgiving. That should give the young folks time to get settled."

Mike laughed, "If I know Wilma, Christmas dinner is already planned. We don't stand a chance, Big Lund. Might as well keep the womenfolk happy."

Big Lund continued easily, "We could leave the upstairs unfinished, but put in a permanent stairway. Two bedrooms downstairs should be enough for the time being," he chuckled. "The screened-in porch could be enclosed some day, I suppose, but it's nice for ocean breezes."

Nora and Wilma joined the men and the old friends rocked gently, while the moon peeked from behind the clouds. The chain saws and hammers had been put away. A quiet came over the sound as the ocean lapped rhythmically at the shoreline.

The gentle conversation flowed freely between friends who were loved and comfortable in each other's presence. "You know, Mike, it is in the valleys of everyday living that the fabric of society is woven by families who love each other and commit themselves to godly living."

Mike nodded. "You're right, Big Lund. I read someplace that man makes life complex. Life is simple and the simple thing is the right thing." He gazed intently at Lund. "Old friend, do you think our children will understand that there is true greatness in simplicity?"

Big Lund rocked quietly as a gust of wind blew across the porch. "I hope so. I truly hope so. We are wealthy men, Mike. We have our homes, our children, our work — and two beautiful, practical women reminding us that tomorrow is the Lord's day. Not necessarily a day of rest — with dinner on the grounds and all-day singing." He smiled across the room at his wife. "It's been a good day. A really good day."

five

Lundy

Although the house still smelled of paint and varnish, the bride and groom were in their home for Christmas. But two years later, on Christmas Eve, 1957, someone special had joined them. Big Lund rocked gently beside the open fire. Cradled in his arms was Lundy — his newborn grandson, Lund Michael Lundstrom.

Melissa, in a red velvet robe with white furry trim, looked like a Christmas angel propped up on a sofa, surrounded by pillows. Four attentive men were at her beck and call, to say nothing of Nora and Wilma.

"Looks like we defied tradition, Nora, having our Christmas Eve dinner here so Melissa and the baby can remain at home," Mike teased as he put chairs around the table. When dinner was ready Big Lund had to be coaxed to put Lundy in the mahogany cradle he had made for him.

Melissa sat like a queen at the foot of the table. Nelson, at the head of his table, reached out to join hands as he thanked God for Christmas, the birthday of the King, and for the birth of his son, Lundy. With deep gratitude he thanked God for his family and home — and blessed the food. Then he grinned and said, "It's hard to believe that two years ago we all had Christmas Eve at the Big House, and then Christmas Day here. What a day! Remember?"

Wilma, carrying in more steaming dishes, added "Who could forget? You around checking the woodwork and we were afraid to walk on these perfectly polished floors. You kept admiring your own work; even Chad dared us to find the seams on the wall paper."

Chad's fiancee, Jean Johnson, laughed with the others. "You mean you all did everything — even the decorating?"

"We'll do the same for you and Chad," Big Lund offered.

Chad nudged Jean, "You can never keep them from discussing their next building plans. You should see the designs in Big Lund's room. He even has drawings from his grandfather in Norway."

"You are all so close," Jean whispered. "I never met a family like yours, and I love it." She reached for his hand.

The Christmas music filled the house, and after the table was cleared and the dishes done, everyone gathered by the fire to hear Big Lund read the Christmas story. Gifts under the tree seemed less important when the beauty of Christmas filled each heart with the reality of the Babe of Bethlehem — Emmanuel, God with us.

In the hush of Christmas Eve, a baby's low cry came from the cradle in the yellow bedroom. Melissa disappeared into the dark and picked up Lundy, awake just in time for the opening of the gifts. Stories poured forth from long ago — until once again Nora and Wilma brought trays of Norwegian Yule bread, cookies, coffee and spiced tea.

"I'm the happiest man in the world," Nels whispered to Melissa as he munched a cookie. "I've got you and Lundy. What more could a man ask?"

Later, they stood arm in arm in the doorway watching the cars pull out of the driveway. They smiled as Big Lund took Nora's hand to cross the lot to the Big House.

When his parents were out of sight, Nelson closed the door. "Merry Christmas, darling," he said to Melissa.

"And a thousand more together?" she asked.

He nodded. They tiptoed quietly into the bedroom where Lundy slept peacefully. *At least I have a thousand dreams and plans,* he thought, *for the three of us.*

six

The Wind

"*L*undy," *Noragram said to me as she pushed herself up from the dining chair, "My how we loved you. You were still so small, so vulnerable."*

I studied Noragram as she shuffled across the polished hardwood floor to the bookcase and back again lugging the musty family album. Her eyes sparkled with the memories of yesteryears as she sat beside me at the table. She turned the pages slowly, reflecting on each photo. Snapshots of my grandfather Big Lund. Pictures of their wedding day back in the thirties. Pictures of their first home. And snaps of Nelson — their only child, my father. Then page after page of the grown Nelson and Melissa, the mother I never knew.

Noragram was chuckling as she looked at my parents' first Christmas together. And then their third Christmas with me in the cradle that Big Lund had made. Then Noragram shook her head sadly, "It's hard to believe it was the last Christmas that Nelson and Melissa would spend together."

I shifted uneasily as Noragram turned the album pages, knowing what was coming. Her forefinger settled on the snapshot of my mother's grave. "Oh, Lundy," she said, "If only you could have known your mother. She was so full of life and dreams." Noragram sighed — a deep, painful sigh. "Your father was proud of her. And Big Lund and I were certain that Nelson had finally settled down, that he'd stay on in the area forever. But then. . ."

"A drunk came along."

"Not just a drunk, Lundy."

"He was drinking," I accused. "Same difference."

She nodded, agreeing reluctantly. "But he was only a young lad — a boy who didn't know that anyone loved him." Her fragile hand touched mine. "I don't think I'll ever forget that September morning in 1958. Your mother had gone to the store to buy a toy for you. She was on her way home. One minute she was walking along the edge of the road in broad daylight and then..."

"Then a car careened out of control and she was hurled into the air, the life sucked out of her," I said scathingly, remembering how my father had described it. "My mother never had a chance."

"Your mother never knew, Lundy," Noragram said softly. "She died instantly."

* * *

The beloved minister, Dr. Parks, looked at the people gathered from the community. His white hair framed a face that told of the anguish of his soul, yet his presence spoke peace.

" 'Let not your heart be troubled. You believe in God, believe also in me. In my Father's house are many mansions. I go to prepare a place you.' " The voice droned on, " 'I am the resurrection and the life. He that believeth in me, though he were dead, yet shall he live.' "

Then with rising crescendo, " 'The Lord is my shepherd . . .' "

Nelson Lundstrom sat rigidly between Nora and Big Lund, the dark night of his soul etched in his grief-stricken face.

Beside them, Mike Newton wept openly, unable to restrain his grief. Wilma held Mike's arm, not only for strength, but to remind him she was there. Her dark eyes looked, but saw nothing. She heard the words, but they slipped away.

Nora sat stonily, listening for some word of comfort. The pain in her heart was like a knife, probing deeper into her soul. She agonized for her son in his grief. Big Lund clung to Nelson's arm.

Nora wondered if they heard the pastor saying, "We are pilgrims in a foreign land going home. Everything we enjoy in this life is but a preview of home. Our grief, our joy, our tears, and our laughter are a part of our pilgrim journey, but we will never feel that we truly belong until we are home — home in God now and with God soon, oh, so soon for some."

Dr. Parks' voice broke. The congregation wept openly. Nelson groaned — the sound of a wounded man, the sound of a distant storm. Nora trembled. Big Lund wrapped his arm around his son.

"Melissa is home." The minister hesitated. "I was so sure that I would go home before our beautiful Melissa. I have waited and prepared for my journey for I knew my days were numbered. Just last Sunday I told Melissa, 'I look for that city, whose builder and maker is God. I look for the lights of home. Sometimes I almost hear the angels sing.' "

Nelson stiffened, his face frozen.

"When I read how God said He would wipe all tears away, I saw the beauty of that love. It was as though He told the angels to step aside, for He reserved the right to wipe our tears. He alone will wipe your tears, Nelson. Somehow, even today, in our hour of grief, God is reaching into your heart, Nelson, and into this community to wipe our tears. Our laughter has been stilled — but only for a time — for deep within our hearts we say with King David when his son died, 'You can't come to me, but I will come to you.' Death is not the end for Melissa. Death is a door to a new beginning for her. All our dreams and hopes can pass away, but God's eternal plan, His everlasting love in us who believe can never pass away.

"Nelson — Wilma — Mike, God's Word says, 'Let not your hearts be troubled.' How is that possible? Now is the time to forgive the young man who caused this grief. God didn't cause this death. Disobedience to God's laws and the laws of society — sin — caused our grief. The young man who chose to disregard the laws of society will have to live with his choice."

Dr. Parks shook his head sadly, "But our hearts can be troubled for a lifetime if we allow hate to fill the empty place of loneliness. We must forgive and pray that the young man will turn to God and be forgiven by Him. He lives with this tragedy, too.

"Pray for one another. When such a tragedy occurs, many people think more about eternity, about how they live each day. They draw closer to God. But some turn inward to nurture hate and unforgiveness. I plead with you to remember the beauty and fragrance of Melissa who grew up among us. She is home! We are the ones who must answer the unspoken question, *How can we live without her?* We can only live by the grace of God. We are powerless to face the grief without Him."

Nelson's sob ripped through the church. Big Lund gripped his shoulder. "My dear ones, you who are Melissa's family, I can offer to you only the truth of God's Word: 'Lo, I am with you always.' I can offer you only the faithfulness of a loving God: 'The Lord is my Shepherd. I shall not want.' He will continue to lead you. I can offer you only the love and prayers of this congregation — the people of the community who love you and who loved Melissa. I can offer you only the peace that passes understanding.

'Fear thou not
For I am with thee
Be not dismayed
For I am thy God
I will strengthen thee;
Yea, I will help thee
Yea, I will uphold thee with
The right hand of my righteousness.'

"I know the hope I give to you is real, for I, too, have learned through grief. Where there has been grief and sorrow, there is also growth and depth. We cannot yield to the luxury of grief, for we will lose our courage and will to live.

"For Melissa's sake — for Jesus' sake, fill the empty place with service to others. Fill the loneliness with gratitude for the joys that you knew. Stretch your soul with forgiveness and compassion. You will then make more room for God Himself.

"Let us leave this place with triumph, not defeat; love, not hate; forgiveness, not bitterness; the peace of God, and not the anguish of the soul.

"As a testimony to Melissa's faith, I am going to ask you to stand and sing The Lord's Prayer together."

The song started softly, voices choked with tears. Nora stared at the face of the pastor. His face glowed as though he could see beyond earth's boundaries.

Our Father, who art in heaven — The music was slow and soft — tender, loving, caring like the Father.

Hallowed be Thy name — An awe seemed to descend over the congregation. *Thy kingdom come. Thy will be done* — Nora could hear the trembling bass of Big Lund. *On earth as it is in heaven.*

The music blended young and older voices. *Give us this day our daily bread. And forgive us our debts.* With choking sobs, Wilma and Mike attempted to sing *As we forgive our debtors.*

Nora glanced at Nelson. He stood silent, rigid, his hands clenched in despair. Big Lund held him tightly.

The music continued, *And lead us not into temptation. But deliver us from evil.*

Nora could almost see the face of the young man whose car had gone out of control. Taking the Newton's daughter from them. Stealing Nelson's beloved Melissa. Silencing Lundy's mother. The youth, too stupified from drinking to comprehend what had happened until he came to in a jail cell.

Nora looked up.

Dr. Parks stretched his arms toward heaven. The swell of voices rose with the organ. Finally, in barely a whisper, Nora joined the singing: *For Thine is the kingdom, and the power, and the glory, forever. Amen.*

The long day had ended. Big Lund and Nels talked long into the night — remembering Melissa. Nora remembered singing The Lord's Prayer while Baby Lundy whimpered in her arms.

* * *

Days later a tropical storm moved in from the ocean.
Storm warnings alerted the residents to prepare for power
failure. No evacuation was advised. Heavy rains and winds
made driving hazardous.

Big Lund disregarded the warnings and edged the truck
out of the driveway. Instinct told him that Nels would be
at Melissa's grave. For the past few days Nels had been
too composed; his controlled silence was frightening.

Lund's heart broke when he found his son kneeling by
the grave, his hands pressed to his face. Fear gripped Lund
as he overheard the muffled words, "Oh, how I hate him
for killing you, my Melissa. My darling Melissa. How can
I ever live without you? How can I ever forgive that man?
My God, help me — but, oh, how I hate him."

Big Lund tugged at Nelson's arm. Finally, with brute
strength, he pulled him from the grave site to the shelter
of the truck. Nels seemed oblivious to the pelting rain.

Back at the house, Big Lund eased the wet clothes off
Nelson as if he were a child. Nelson shivered but Big Lund
knew it was not so much from the storm without as from
the raging storm within. Reluctantly Nelson stretched out
on the bed in his boyhood room. He was exhausted, heartbro-
ken. He seemed unaware that King, the Shepherd dog,
nuzzled his hand, nor did he hear the sounds of his son
Lundy crying in the other room.

Hours later, Nora stole into the bedroom and pulled the
quilt over her restless, sleeping son. Baby Lundy slept in
Nels's old crib beside Big Lund in the master bedroom.
King lay curled by the fireplace. But Nora, wide awake and
alone, paced the house and prayed for her fragmented family.

Outside, the angry winds matched the churning sea. It
would be a long night. Across the road, Melissa Lundstrom's
house stood dark and empty in the roaring, gusty wind.

seven

Miss Lottie

Noragram's sigh cut across the dining room; her eyes were misty.

"It's okay, Grams," I told her. "We can talk again later — tomorrow perhaps."

"No, Lundy. When you're eighty-plus, you don't have too many tomorrows. Some of this talking is long overdue."

"It does help," I admitted, "knowing how Dad really felt."

"Lundy, he was devastated when your mother died. For weeks, he went to the grave every day. We couldn't make him understand that Melissa wasn't really there — just her body. Heaven seemed so unreal to Nelson. And then one day in February, a few months after your mother's death, Nelson packed up and left Wrightsville forever."

"That's when he left for the Navy Air Force?"
"Yes."
"And that's when he left me behind," I said bitterly.

* * *

Late spring — May, 1961. It had been two years since Nelson went away — and he had not been home in that time. Nora worked quietly in her garden. The pampas grass rustled in the breeze, flowing in from the ocean. As she worked, her thoughts were on her son and grandson — would Nelson and Lundy always be apart?

Weeds and thoughts need pulling, she mused, *and I can't allow fear and worry to grow in my mind.* Snatching a tough weed, she pulled the top off. *Looks like this one takes my digger — can't leave the root.*

Big Lund, carrying a tray with coffee mugs and raisin toast, coaxed Nora to stop a few minutes. Wiping her hands on her apron, she sat down at the wrought iron table. Together they drank coffee in silence.

They watched the robins in the ripening strawberry patch. "Nelson could never get enough," Nora thought out loud. "How I do miss him, but he'll soon be home. Perhaps he'll find a good wife — one who would love Lundy. How good it would be to see Melissa's house full of living again."

"Having Lundy with us has almost been like watching Nelson grow up again — except Lundy has so much of Melissa in him. Seems more sensitive than our Nels. Look at him, will you!"

Suddenly Lundy was racing down the walkway to his friend, Miss Lottie. Big Lund rose to meet them — Miss Lottie, tapping her cane, with Missy, her old German shepherd, ambling along and Lundy, pulling a wagon hauling pieces of lumber. King welcomed them all with a round of barking.

"I'm going to build a house, like Big Lund," Lundy announced.

"While you and Nora talk, Miss Lottie, we men have work to do." Big Lund and Lundy walked off across the yard, hand in hand.

"Look at those two, will you. I tell you, Nora, that youngun follows Big Lund like a shadow. Hard to believe he will be four in December. That one is a knowing child. Talks like a grownup, no baby talk for him."

"Guess he has only us old folks to play with, and Big Lund carries on a conversation like he could be Nelson." She handed Miss Lottie a cup of coffee.

"Coffee tastes mighty good about this time," Miss Lottie said, slurping loudly. "Have you heard from Wilma and Mike lately? How I miss them — good friends — just like family."

Nora's eyes misted. "Our world turned upside down after Melissa died. Even though I know God works all things for good, it still is such a mystery. For months after the funeral, I heard the pounding hammers, but missed the ringing of the men's laughter. What I wouldn't give to hear Nelson laugh again! You know how it was, Miss Lottie, Big Lund and Mike tried to keep the business going at the same pace, but Nelson just withdrew. I tried to encourage him to spend time with little Lundy, but he just stared at him, like he was a stranger. It was as if he couldn't love him, even if he had wanted to. Then one day, Miss Lottie, when Lundy was little more than a year old, Nelson just said, 'I've got to get away. I'm joining the Naval Air Corps. I can't do Lundy any good now. Could you please take care of him? Perhaps later I can be a real father.' "

Miss Lottie waited. She knew Nora had to say what was in her heart before she could answer her question.

"He just wouldn't listen to reason. He was numb, Miss Lottie, he really was." Nora wiped her eyes. "Overnight! Our boy just changed overnight, and I know it's the hate and bitterness that is still destroying him."

"But Nora, you must never lose hope. A weed grows overnight, but an oak takes a long time. We can pray for Nelson, but we also need to teach little Lundy all we can. We don't know what the future holds for him."

Nora smiled. "Last week I overheard Big Lund tell him about the trees in the forest growing tall and strong. Lundy listened like a grown child while Big Lund explained how the cold mountain climate produced good, hard wood. Then he said that grief and sorrow also produce strong people — like trees. Palm trees grow in the desert, and cedars in the mountains. He just talks as though the boy understands."

"Perhaps he does." I heard little Lundy ask, 'What kind of a tree is my daddy?'"

"I told you, Nora, that child is a knowing child. He told me all about his mother — even told me he forgave the man who killed her."

"But, Miss Lottie, he isn't four yet."

"I know, but listen to this. I asked him how he knew to forgive the man who killed his mother. He answered 'Because Big Lund did. I want to be like Big Lund.' Now tell me, Nora, have you ever heard a child with such wisdom? I have to laugh at how he calls you Noragram instead of Grandma Nora. And insists on calling his grandfather, Big Lund. Then he tells me, 'I am little Lundy, and Grandpa is Big Lund. Someday, I'll be Big Lund.'"

"We're so thankful to have Lundy with us," Nora said. "As for Wilma and Mike, I never saw such strength emerge from those two. Mike did all he could to help our Nels. He put aside his own heartbreak to talk to Nels."

"I miss them Newtons," Miss Lottie said. "I just felt so bad when they moved away."

"I did hear from them last week. They've settled into the new house in Richmond. It's not all that far to Virginia, we'll have to go up for a weekend sometime soon. They keep hoping that by spring they can come back to the beach. But with Mike's brother sick, Mike just had to take over the family lumber company. It really is best that Mike and Wilma went right away, to keep things together."

Miss Lottie rocked thoughtfully, "It's just like them Newtons to help someone."

Nora smiled. "Wilma never guessed that her philosophy, 'The best way to deal with grief is to get busy and help someone else,' would be put to work so dramatically. But she does say that the old hurts are healing as she reaches out to Mike's family."

Lottie tapped her cane. "Been some powerful changes since Melissa left us — mostly for good, though, since people's faith grows stronger in trouble. Then again, for some, like Nelson, the grief goes inside. And then I've been mighty troubled to hear about our organist, Jean, giving back the ring to Chad. Nora, what's wrong with young

45

folks? Wonder what they want? Heard tell the child's mother wanted her to travel in Europe. Some famous violinist asked her to play the piano for him. Huh! Sounds like the mother cooking up a romance. I don't like the idea much. Oh, the mother is going along; it looks better that way. But I think she wants to get Jean away from Chad — not good enough — huh! They should have been married two years ago."

For a minute, Nora tried to block out the endless chatter, but she heard Miss Lottie saying, "By the way, Nora, been meaning to ask you — What happened to the boy who killed Melissa?"

Nora bit her lip. *How many times had Miss Lottie asked the same question over the last years?* But more patiently than she felt, she answered, "It was Wilma who suggested to Mike that they visit the boy and talk to him. He was only sixteen — lonely. No friends. A broken home. The car was even stolen. But on their third visit, the boy broke down and sobbed like a child and begged them to forgive him. The judge said he hadn't seen anything like it before, but he granted Mike's request to have the boy paroled to him.

Miss Lottie's eyes brightened. "Now I remember. He works in the lumber business with Mike in the summer and attends the university. Funny how I keep forgetting." Miss Lottie's wrinkled face looked up to the sky, "But, Oh Lord, our Nelson hasn't forgiven. Help our boy, Nelson." Then she turned to Nora. "He will, Nora. God will deliver."

"If only it didn't take so long," Nora whispered back.

"Come, Missy, time to go." Miss Lottie poked the dog with her cane. That old dog's getting mighty lazy these days. She misses Jake, she does. I miss him too. Sixty years we celebrated. My, Nora, we did have a party, didn't we?" She leaned over the porch rail and waved at Lundy. "Look at that child, Nora, walks just like Big Lund."

Nora watched Miss Lottie go down the road tapping her cane and singing, "I'll fly away, oh glory, I'll fly away."

eight

The Parade

"*Lundy, it was over five years before your father came home from the service.*" *Noragram was pensive as she ran her hand over the pictures in the photo album — snapshot after snapshot of Nelson in uniform. "Your dad liked being a Navy pilot," she said. He liked the excitement of flying."*

"Did he like Vietnam?" I asked.

She smiled wanly. "It was never a popular war, Lundy, even in those early years. He just did what he had to do."

"Yeah," I answered. "He did what he liked doing. Flying his A4 Skyhawk off the aircraft carrier and streaking up the Gulf of Tonkin, flak bursting all around him. Anything but be at home rearing his son." The coldness in my own voice surprised me.

"We almost lost him, Lundy, but I didn't know that until he got home."

"Almost lost him?" I repeated. "Dad never said anything about that."

47

"It wasn't his favorite topic. Nelson crashed on a return flight, trying to land on the U.S.S. Constellation."

"You mean he ditched at sea? Is that when he was injured?"

She nodded. "But in spite of the injury, Nelson was one of the lucky ones. Three months after Nelson's accident, his buddy was the first American shootdown of the war. By that time Nelson was back in the States, still recovering."

"Was that the year of the parade? The year he met Helen?"

"Yes," Noragram said softly. "In the spring of 1964."

* * *

Wilmington, North Carolina came alive in the spring. Dogwood and azaleas burst from tiny buds and wrapped the city in soft garments of pastel lace. Stately magnolia trees stood guard over the manicured lawns, and pines stretched to the sky to welcome the warmth and color of spring.

Tourists came from far and near, forgetting the winds of winter to tour gardens and homes and to attend luncheons and dinner parties. Sailboats, with colorful masts, filled the sound. Cape Fear River swelled with pride as history was recalled.

The great battleship U.S.S. North Carolina sounded her guns and sent lights flashing across Cape Fear River.

Movie stars and beauty queens reigned like royalty — attending concerts and parties — to the delight of the Wilmington society. City officials and visiting dignitaries joined the celebrities to wave from their flower-decorated cars.

The shops along the parade route were filled with people watching from second story windows. The crowds below craned their necks to see the marching bands, prancing horses, antique cars and the garden floats with beautiful girls waving to the crowd. Riding on the back seat of one shiny, white Cadillac was a shy Navy officer and the beauty queen from Arizona.

As they rode by, the excited voice of a child cried out. "There he is! There's my daddy! Daddy, Daddy!" Hoisted high on Big Lund's shoulders, Lundy Lundstrom waved frantically at the Navy pilot sitting beside the beautiful woman with black hair and flashing eyes.

"Who is that adorable little boy, Nelson?" she asked. "Why is he looking at you?"

"Daddy, Daddy," the child called again.

Nelson waved back. Helen Thornton threw him a kiss.

"That boy, Helen, is my son."

"Whew! You are indeed a mystery man. First Chad Newton tells me that you are a hero — you flew numerous dangerous missions. Now, you tell me you have a son? Where is your wife?"

Nelson tensed. "She's dead! Didn't Chad tell you? She was killed five years ago."

"Oh, Nelson, I'm sorry. No, I didn't know. But you are alive, Nels, and five years is a long time. You need to live again!" Helen reached for his hand and determined that she would make this silent hero come alive. They rode in silence but Helen kept thinking, *All the men in my life came crawling, promising me the moon.* She smiled to herself. *But this one is different. I want him and Dad always says I get what I want.* She was pleased that she had managed to get her wish to go to Europe fulfilled. What an added bonus — to meet Jean Johnson and Pierre, the violinist, and get an invitation to Wilmington and the Azalea Festival.

Helen smiled at the crowd and waved, then reached for her escort's hand again. A warm surge went through her when he gripped her hand firmly in his own. With a fierce determination she vowed to make this man alive — and hers. She would wing this hero pilot to earth, but she knew she would have to be careful. This was no ordinary man that she wanted. She was tired of the others, the socially acceptable ones her mother chose for her or the ones who wanted her money. This one, she knew, would please her father. Her dad could be impressed with a hero. This Nelson Lundstorm — this strong silent, mysterious man — this one she wanted! She remembered reading someplace that a passionate man has potential for greatness. Her instincts told her that this blond Norwegian, silent and mysterious, had strength and passion.

The crowds were cheering. The Marine band played. Helen smiled and waved — but her thoughts ran wild. This invitation to the Azalea Festival wasn't as boring as she had anticipated. She was glad she listened to the Wilmington historian tell about the beginning of the festival in 1934 when Houston Moore decided Wilmington needed a festival spirit after the Great Depression. In the first festival, there were thirty-one floats, five bands and two military marching units. But the festival had grown to include sailing regatta, powerboat races, horse shows, tours and endless floats.

Helen's cultural background made her a good listener, even if she was inwardly bored. Now she was glad she had listened to the old dowager. It could come in handy knowing about local tradition. *I wonder what Nelson's family is like? I'll have to play up to the child. That will take some doing, but he certainly looked adorable on his grandfather's shoulders.*

Helen and Nelson waved. His hand closed tightly over hers. Her fingers intertwined his gently, seductively. It had been a long time since any man excited her like this one.

Nelson's thoughts tumbled together. *I have to get out! Five years in the service is enough. I've done my duty. I'm too restless. I need something new. I don't seem to settle any place.* Across his mind came pictures of Lundy waving, and a wave of guilt engulfed him. He had to make it up somehow. Then the nightmare came again: Melissa's grave, the ocean. The years with the Navy Air Force. The escalating involvement in Viet Nam. And now the endless parties, the parade. *At least being an escort to this beautiful girl isn't as boring as I thought it would be.*

Helen was right. Melissa was dead and he was alive. Why did he feel so dead? *How I wish I could feel again. Been numb so long-so long. All those reconnaissance missions. They thought I was brave. I was a coward — just wanted to die. I couldn't even die! Just wounded. Nothing more.*

The crowds cheered! Nelson and Helen waved. He was aware of the warmth of Helen next to him, the tantalizing perfume, the shine of her black hair — and those dark eyes! He moved closer, a hunger growing inside of him.

She withdrew her hand to wave, then turned her dark eyes to him. He saw her soft mouth and suddenly wanted to kiss her.

She held his hand, caressing it slowly. Nelson tensed!

Strange how he suddenly really noticed her. Where had he been all these days, escorting her all over town? He knew he wanted to be alone with this beauty. No one had stirred his emotions like this one. As the parade ended, he said, "Let's walk on the beach before we have dinner with my family." His voice sounded husky and far away. "We can go to the party later."

She leaned closer, "Let me change into my sport clothes first."

His thoughts whirled. How he despised social functions. He needed the ocean, the sound of the waves and the sand on his feet — and he needed this girl in his arms.

He cringed for a moment, realizing how Helen Thornton had charmed her way into Wilmington society. All those mothers introducing her to their sons — just as mothers had tried to interest him in their daughters; they finally gave up. He thought of the admiring glances that followed Helen. She smiled at them all. He spoke his thoughts before he realized it. "You certainly charmed Wilmington, Helen. Even upstaged the local beauty queens. Let's go to the beach as fast as possible. You'll love the ocean — it's the best part of North Carolina."

It seemed to take forever to escape the crowds for the open expanse of sand and sky. The ocean ebbed and flowed with her own rhythm. The seagulls screeched a welcome.

Helen and Nelson walked hand in hand along Wrightsville Beach. This was a new world to Helen, and something of the ocean's spell, the peace, and rhythm eased into her restless, impetuous nature. She sensed a strange awe. This was Nelson's world — just as mysterious as he was. She meant to hold this moment forever. It was new and gripping.

Nelson's thoughts were jumping like the waves. He was aware of Helen's low cut blouse against her soft tan skin. Her dark hair and eyes shone with intensity against the dazzling white clouds and blue skies above.

The last days were running together, days he had spent with this beautiful woman. How could he forget Melissa? He felt guilt, then rage against the one who had destroyed her life, his life. But now, he suddenly felt alive — a wild passion screaming for release. He felt like a man again!

Helen moved closer. This man she wanted! No man had ever stirred such passion within her. She meant to have him. She had never been denied anything. No matter what her mother, Abigail, thought, she would have Nelson Lundstrom. She could handle her father, Edward Thornton.

Nelson felt the passion in her as they walked barefoot in the sand. Helen felt the rising depth of feeling in Nelson — then slipped from his grasp to chase sea gulls, daring him to follow. Nelson ran after her, caught her up in his arms and hungrily reached for her warm lips. Helen was trembling as their lips met. Somewhere, deep within her, the ocean touched the sky.

nine

A Knowing Child

Four weeks later in May, 1964, Nora and Big Lund watched the plane, carrying Nelson, Helen, and Lundy, dip behind clouds to streak over the New Hanover airport and disappear into the sky.

As they drove home from the airport, Big Lund and Nora felt the weight of their years. Like a fast-moving drama the past days had moved across the stage, with Helen Thornton the leading lady.

When they walked into the Big House, the silence engulfed them. Nora put on the coffee pot, and, within minutes, the familiar sound of Miss Lottie's cane broke the stillness.

"Saw you drive up — thought maybe you'd have the coffee pot on. And thought you might need a little lovin'." Miss Lottie looked anxiously into the face of her old friends — and waited.

Nora was crying when she said, "Strange that I should feel sad, when the very thing I prayed for has come to pass. All these years we've been praying for a wife for Nels and a mother for Lundy. Oh, it was so good to hear Nels laugh again and tell his old stories — almost like it used to be."

Big Lund interrupted, "We couldn't help but like Helen, like a fountain of youth, bubbling like a spring. She wouldn't let Nelson out of her sight. But I can't help but wonder what her family is like. She didn't say much, just that her father was in land development and that Nelson would love the challenge of the West as soon as he was out of the service."

Miss Lottie chuckled, "Imagine our Nels eloping! Last person in the world to take us all by surprise. Never dreamed he wouldn't stay right here, but then again maybe he needs to get away from all the old memories. Some folks say that's the best way — just get away from them memories. But," she said, running on, "I always had a knowing that hurts be best settled where the hurting began. Heard a preacher once say that God has to get the storm out of us, before He gets us out of the storm."

Big Lund gazed over the ocean, his thoughts on the boy who had followed him like a shadow. As though to convince himself, he said, "It was good to see Nels take a new interest in the boy, and Helen seemed to take to our Lundy. I guess they are right, the boy needs young parents."

Nora sighed. "Helen promised that Lundy would have everything he ever wanted, even a swimming pool. Then, of course, we'll visit often, and they'll come here, too. Wilma and Mike will want to see Lundy, too. Chad reminded us that planes do fly between Arizona and Wilmington." She sighed again. "It sure was good to hear Nelson laugh."

Miss Lottie stood up. "Come on, Missy, these folks need to get some rest and it's time for us old folks to settle down. Just don't forget, Nora, our heavenly Father still watches over us. We can pray."

With that parting word, Miss Lottie tapped her cane down the road, and Missy ambled along beside her. "I'll fly away," echoed in the wind. Big Lund smiled, and closed the door for the night.

Miss Lottie began talking out loud to her dog. "Looks like we're going to have to get used to the quiet, Missy — Lundy gone and all. Wonder how it is that some things seem so right, yet feel so wrong. Maybe I'm just a meddlesome old woman, but something inside my old bones wants to have a good cry. Well, Missy, you old lazybones, what do you think? I know you miss Lundy, too. Reckon some changes coming down the road?"

She talked on as they continued making their way home. "It is true, haven't seen Nelson so happy since his first wedding day. Lord have mercy. He just grabbed me up and hugged me — 'Miss Lottie, I just married the most beautiful girl in the world. Helen, I want you to meet the most loved granny on the sound — the one and only Miss Lottie.'

"You didn't like her, did you, Missy? Shame on you, growling at that pretty girl, plumb scared her to death. Her prettier than a movie star, and no wonder Nelson couldn't take his eyes off her. Seemed mighty fond of Lundy, too.

"Been mighty troublesome to have Lundy come running to me when he heard the news. 'Miss Lottie, Miss Lottie, they're taking me to Arizona to boarding school. Daddy said Nora and Big Lund are too old to take care of me. Are they? You aren't too old, are you? And what's a boarding school?'

"That's when I held that child real close like, on my lap. We just rocked a spell, but that's when I felt a cloud coming across the sun.

"I told him how the tide ebbs and flows, how God has a plan for each one. Man might have dreams, but God has a plan."

Lottie stopped for a rest and patted the old dog's head affectionately. "You might be old, lazy bones, but you make a mighty good listener. Fact is, Missy, I'd rather talk to you than some folks I know." She chuckled with delight. The old dog wagged her tail and nudged her nose against Lottie's legs.

"Remember the day Lundy chased a butterfly through Nora's bean patch? Big Lund showed him how he had pulled all the beans up. Then they planted more beans, but Big Lund told Lundy that sometimes people chase a butterfly and forget what's really important. I reminded Lundy of that story and, being the knowing child he is, I think he understood. Then I said, 'Right now Lundy, the important things for you are to obey your father, study and learn.

Never forget what Big Lund and Nora taught you. Even if your life is different, you can't chase butterflies, wishing for things that used to be. Just remember the important things. Don't ever forget the ocean, how the tide ebbs and flows. Someday you'll return Lundy Boy. You'll come back.' "

Miss Lottie walked onto her porch and then sat and rocked quietly, reliving the conversation with Lundy. She could see his thoughtful eyes looking into her face. "I'll never forget you, Miss Lottie. Nora and Big Lund either. I'll be good, but I already know that Helen only pretends she likes me because she likes my daddy."

The cane tapped furiously arousing Missy. "Happy, is he? Nelson is happy. Since when is happiness a goal? Oh, Nelson, my boy, happiness is fleeting, but true joy comes from God. Don't chase butterflies and stomp on what's really worthwhile."

The dark clouds gathered over the ocean while the pine trees swayed in the wind. A screen door slammed. "Come on, Missy, storm coming." Miss Lottie closed the door on another day while the clouds rode on the wind.

ten

The Thorntons

*N*oragram closed the photo album and pushed it to the center of the old oak table. She patted it as though it were an old friend. "Lundy," she asked, "do you remember the day you left Big Lund and me?"

` "Remember?" I repeated, choking on the memory. "I thought you and Big Lund didn't want me anymore."

"Didn't want you!" Noragram cried out. "Letting you go was the hardest thing we ever did, even harder than saying goodbye to your beloved mother."

"And I thought you were punishing me."

"Punishing you," she exclaimed, tears welling in her eyes. "How? Why?"

"It was right after I chased a butterfly through your bean patch. Big Lund was so mad when he showed me all the beans I had pulled up. I thought maybe . . ." I paused, not wanting to hurt her. "I really thought Big Lund was still mad at me so you were sending me away."

"Oh, dear Lundy," she said. "We loved you too much to send you away. We only let you go because Helen and

Nelson were so certain you'd be happier. They convinced us you'd have everything you needed."

* * *

Lundy bit his lips and sat stiffly beside his father on the airplane. The earth below looked like a patchwork quilt of mountains and villages brought together by ribbons of highways and the cars looked like crawling ants. Then the plane climbed into the fairyland of make believe. Lundy's imagination built castles in the clouds, just as he had built castles in the ocean sands.

Nelson and Helen were engrossed in each other, oblivious to Lundy. Lundy clenched his fists, swinging his legs restlessly. He wanted to cry — and to fly right back to Noragram and Big Lund. Then he heard the couple across the aisle talking.

"What a lucky guy," murmured the elderly man, casting a glance toward Nelson and his bride.

"Don't be too sure, Albert Cranston," his wife smiled back. "When they've been married twenty-five years, we'll know how lucky he is. Patting the old man's knee affectionately, she whispered, "We are the lucky ones. The logs in our fireplace have kept a steady warmth, not a blazing fire that is too hot to be near — just cozy and comforting."

"You're right, of course, Sarah, but a man is old when he stops looking," he teased, "and that woman is enough to stop traffic. The man looks rather reserved, though, and she doesn't seem his type. The boy looks like him — must be a second marriage."

"You're always the engineer, trying to figure things out. That boy reminds me of Craig's little Bert — got to be six or seven. But there *is* something sad about the child. I wish I could get his attention."

When Lundy looked across the aisle, Sarah Cranston smiled and said, "Hello there." Reaching into her bag, Sarah pulled out some pictures. "I have a grandson, just about your age. His name is Bert. Would you like to see pictures?"

Nelson nodded his approval, and within moments Lundy was sitting with the Cranstons, looking at photos and listening to stories about Sarah's grandson.

"My gramma's name is Noragram. That's my dad and stepmother," he whispered confidentially. "My real mother was killed in a car accident, and Noragram and Big Lund took care of me until my dad came home from the Navy. I didn't want to leave them."

Impulsively, Sarah drew him to her. He buried his head in her shoulder and she felt his quiet tears.

"Be brave," Sarah whispered. "I know your grandparents love you very much. Your daddy loves you, too, and I'm sure he'll take good care of you."

After a few moments, Lundy raised his head. "You can call me Lundy-boy, that's what Noragram and Big Lund call me. I'm named for Big Lund. Helen calls me *that child*." He paused a minute, then said, "She likes my daddy and he wants me with him now. Big Lund said I must be a good boy and obey my daddy."

"Your grandpa is right," Sarah Cranston assured him.

Sarah Cranston began then to tell Lundy some stories. The one he liked the best was about the Good Shepherd and the lost sheep. Lundy fell asleep dreaming about the sheep who had wandered away and smiled when the Shepherd found them. Then he was himself — small and frightened — among the sheep until the Shepherd reached out and took his hand. He snuggled against his new-found friend Sarah and went on dreaming that he was safe at home in the Big House with Noragram and Big Lund.

Across the aisle, Nelson smiled his approval. The lady looked like she knew how to handle a child. He hadn't seen the tears on his son's face; and now the little boy was sleeping.

Nelson was sure that Helen would be a good mother, but being a good parent was new to both of them. At first he had been reluctant to take Lundy with them. "After we're settled, I'll send for the boy," he had suggested to her.

"No," she had insisted. "The more quickly he adjusts, the better. We have servants who will take care of him and my parents will be his grandparents, too."

Nelson had been so grateful, believing that Helen wanted Lundy with them.

* * *

At the Phoenix airport, as they stepped into the terminal lobby, Helen exclaimed, "There they are."

She was off at once, rushing toward her father's open arms. Mrs. Thornton was more reserved in her welcome. Helen knew it was a sign of disapproval for the hasty elopement to a man Helen hadn't even brought home and introduced to her. But Helen caught a glimpse of admiration in her mother's face when Helen formally introduced her to the tall handsome Norwegian, Nelson Lund Lundstrom. Abigail Thornton could rise to any occasion, and now she assumed her role of a gracious hostess.

Edward Thornton — tall, composed, wealthy — greeted his new son-in-law with the quiet dignity of a man who was used to being in control. Only Helen, his beautiful, spoiled daughter, remained beyond that control, but never beyond his love. Momentarily his dark eyes met Nelson's in a silent challenge. Mentally Nelson shifted into a "battle alert" and grasped the hand of the handsome white-haired executive. While making polite conversation Nelson instinctively knew that, in this situation, the winners would be two beautiful women, whose charms neither man could resist.

Lundy shook hands with the older couple and remembered what Big Lund told him, "When you are in a strange situation stay very still and wait. Don't interrupt adults." No one talked to him, so Lundy knew he would have to be *very* quiet. In his quietness he began to grow lonely.

He remembered that Noragram had said she and Big Lund would always be near him, because love knew no distance. He wanted to feel their love now, and he wished they were close enough to touch. He walked close to his father and took his hand, but he still felt alone, his father still felt far away. Some things were hard to understand. He would be very quiet.

The grown-ups kept talking until a man with a black cap took their bags and helped everyone into a black car. When they arrived at the Thornton estate, the driver opened the doors and said, "Welcome home, Miss Helen."

Lundy held out his hand to shake hands, just like Big

60

Lund said, but the man was too busy to notice him. Now Lundy grew even lonelier, as lonely as he was the night his father and Helen came home and announced, "Congratulate us! We just got married!" That was when Lundy's world changed, but he had never dreamed they would take him away from Noragram and Big Lund. "Don't forget, you are a strong, big Norwegian, Lund Michael Lundstrom," Big Lund had said, but when Helen had jerked him away from Noragram he had forgotten he was strong and he had cried like a baby. Well, he wouldn't do that anymore — cry in front of Helen.

When they reached the sliding glass doors that led out to a patio and swimming pool, Lundy's eyes sparkled. Palm trees and prickly cactus surrounded the flower beds. A marbled fountain bubbled over into a pond of lily pads and gold fish. Mountains loomed in the distance. The cloudless deep blue sky made the world look like a fairy land. Lundy knew his father was impressed by the way he squeezed his hand, too tightly, and drew in his breath.

"Well, well, since you are in the family, my boy," he heard Mr. Thornton address his father like a child, "we might as well offer our congratulations. You know the old saying, 'If you can't fight them, join them.' Believe me, there is no fighting my women. The quicker you learn that, the better." Edward's words didn't seem funny.

They were sitting on the patio now while a woman in a gray and white dress served drinks from a silver tray. Another tray held all kinds of bite-sized food balanced on toothpicks. Lundy wondered what Nora would say about that. She didn't like Big Lund using a toothpick at the table.

Even now, no one noticed Lundy except the Indian gardener. His shiny black shoulder-length hair framed a sun-wrinkled brown face. His large black eyes looked gently at Lundy. "Young man, would you like to see the bird house I built for Miss Helen a long time ago?"

Lundy looked questioningly toward Nels.

"By all means, Kips, take the child," Helen answered. When Lundy waited for his father's permission, Helen snapped, "I said you could go."

Lundy's gaze darted back to his father. Nelson gave a

61

quick nod. With a polite, "Thank you, sir," Lundy turned and took the gardener's hand.

As they walked away, Lundy heard his father say, "He'll be okay. He's a chip off the Big Lund."

Kips took Lundy around the corner of the patio to the kitchen door. After disappearing for a minute, he came back with a tray of lemonade and cookies. They sat down together on the big rocks in the garden in view of the bird house and munched their cookies.

"My name is Tomanto," the Indian said, "but Miss Helen calls me Kips. You can call me Kips if you like. And you, young man, what is your name?"

"My name is Lund Michael Lundstrom," Lundy said proudly. "But Noragram and Big Lund call me Lundy-Boy. My father calls me Lundy. But Helen mostly calls me *that child*." Moments later he was happily telling his new friend about Noragram and North Carolina.

When he started to yawn, Kips crooned a strange song about mountains and buffalo, fishing and hunting. Lundy fell asleep with his head on Kips's lap listening to the songs of the Hopi Indians. Kips gently placed Lundy on the lounge chair and quietly worked around the west patio flower beds, keeping a steady eye on the sleeping boy and thinking back...

Helen had given him the name of Kips when he first came to work for the Thorntons more than twenty-five years ago.

"That's a strange name," Edward Thornton told his daughter. "His name is really Tomanto."

"It's not really strange, Daddy," she had answered saucily, "It stands for *k*ind *I*ndian, *p*oor and *s*toic. He certainly is a kind Indian, Daddy. And he hasn't got any money and he never smiles."

Teena, Tomanto's wife, resented the name, but Tomanto had said, "I do not mind. I am proud to be an Indian. And I am kind and poor and stoic." Then he had laughed. "Besides, my lovely princess, I need this job so we can earn money — so I can someday be free to be an artist."

She had nodded, submitting to him, and padded quietly away in her moccasins.

Helen's shrill voice interrupted the quiet. "Keep an eye

on *that child* and see that he doesn't get into trouble, Kips. We are going across the gardens to see the new house Daddy is building."

"Yes, Miss Helen, the child will stay with me. I'll have Teena prepare his supper early and get him to his room."

As Edward and Abigail Thornton left the house with Nelson and Helen, Kips relaxed. He put aside his garden tools and pulled out his pipe. It had been a long day, getting the patio, gardens, and hanging baskets in perfect order for the return of the newly-weds. His own beloved Teena was preparing the cook-out. When the boy awakened, Kips would return to his cottage, shower and change into a chef hat and coat. But now it was quiet, and a perfect time to rest and watch his beloved mountains in the golden sunset.

The Thornton gardens were really an extention of the indoors. Edward Thornton enjoyed his breakfast on the east patio, where he leisurely read his newspapers. As a young child Helen had demanded that she eat with her father on the patio and not in the dining room or with her mother, in her bedroom. Kips sighed. They had all spoiled the beautiful dark-eyed curly-haired Helen. She'd been too young when she'd learned to charm her way in and out of trouble. He glanced at Lundy. It would take wisdom to maneuver around Helen so she would give the daily order, "Kips, take care of the child!"

"You let Miss Helen order you around like a child, Tomanto," Teena had always complained.

"I know, I know," he would answer patiently, "but I still think of her as a child who manages to twist me around her little finger."

"Ha," retorted Teena. "Men are so stupid sometimes." Affectionately she patted Tomanto's arm, "But you are not stupid, my wise one, for you alone can turn Miss Helen around your way."

When he thought of his Teena, Kips smiled to himself, and his Indian heart told him this child would need a friend. He must be doubly careful. Teena might be jealous since they had no children of their own. He remembered the wisdom of his old grandfather, Chief Great Wind, who had allowed him to sit beside him during village conferences.

"Listen," he said. "Don't talk. When a man is silent he may be thought foolish, but when he opens his mouth he removes all doubt. Measure words carefully, my son, for in the tongue is life or death. Man can gather knowledge like the shells on the beach. Tides of time will come in and go out and take the shells. Wisdom lies deep like the silent palace of the sea where the sand sleeps undisturbed by the ebb and flow of life.

"Times are changing," he had added with sadness. "Listen to the white man, but do not forfeit the wisdom of your fathers for new babbling knowledge. My child, you have the gift of greatness in you, but this gift will be shared only if you are wise. Be patient. I will not live to see the day, but eventually you will be known as one of the great artists of our time. On the canvas you will bring our people to life. Our traditions will not be lost."

Not long after he'd said those words, Chief Great Wind had died sitting in his council seat, his white head bowed. Tomanto felt the darkness of lonely grief.

Kips roused from his memories, watched the sleeping child, his curly blond hair damp on his forehead. Young and vulnerable, he was curled up on the lounge chair, with his thumb in his mouth. The old gardener's eyes were tender, yet a sadness settled over his weathered face.

For thirty years he had served the Thorntons quietly but in his heart he held his grandfather's words, his own dream of being recognized as a gifted artist.

When Lundy awakened Kips promised to show him the bird house. "But first we get you settled in your new room. Miss Helen has asked me to help you and now you must meet my Teena."

Teena's black eyes were expressionless in her dark round face. Her long black hair hung in two thick braids. She refused the modern look although she reluctantly wore the gray and white uniform — with moccasins on her feet. Twenty-eight years ago she had married Tomanto and joined him in the white cottage on the back of the gardens. Together they had tilled the vegetable gardens and sat under their porch roof to watch the beloved mountains and dream of the valley beyond.

Teena looked long at the child, then suddenly something stirred within her — perhaps the longing for the child she never had, or perhaps it was simply the presence of youth. Tomanto watched shrewdly, for his faithful wife was a strong, stubborn woman. He would never cause her needless grief. He watched the tenderness steal into her impassive face and her brown arms reach for the child. She held Lundy close and when he heard strange Indian words — a crooning kind of welcome — he knew he had a friend. Here he could cry if he had to, and here he would be loved.

"Come," Teena urged, "we get you settled in your room and change clothes before the cook-out. You can help my Tomanto start the big grill and put the chairs on the west patio."

Lundy's new bedroom was a large, spacious room overlooking the gardens below. The mountains in the distance looked like sentinals guarding the city. He had lived by the ocean and visited the Blue Ridge Mountains and remembered Grandfather Mountain and the Tweetsee Railroad. This was another world. His small room in Nora's house looked out over the sound and at night he heard the ocean rhythmically rolling in and out. He missed his old toys. Helen had refused to bring "junk" and had promised to buy him new toys — anything he wanted. But right now he only wanted his old familiar friends.

When Lundy saw Kips emerging from the cottage, dressed in a white coat and trousers and wearing a high chef hat, he forgot his fears and burst into laughter. In turn, Kips made a smaller hat from a paper bag and together they arranged the west patio chairs for the evening cook-out. Teena went to the kitchen to oversee the dinner. The younger maids came and went, but for years Teena had seen to it that the household ran smoothly. Although Helen bossed Tomanto in her childish and impish way, Tomanto understood her and skillfully managed to out-maneuver her. Not so with Teena. The two women frequently drew battle lines, but both were wise enough to retreat before open conflict. Helen knew she would lose her faithful Kips if she crossed Teena. Teena stood her ground up to a point and then backed off, for she knew that their secure positions enabled them to save for the day when Tomanto could paint full time. Not even Helen knew of this dream, but Teena was determined to make it come true.

The Thorntons and Lundstroms returned from their tour of the new house built by Thornton's Land Development Enterprises. The company was started by Helen's grandfather who had envisioned a desert city in which indoor and outdoor living harmoniously blended together. He dreamed his dreams and drew his plans for a future that made the old-timers smile. Tomanto's father, Chief Great Wind, had been great friends with Adrian Thornton, "The Old Dreamer," and they had spent many an evening talking of the future — of the white man and of the Indian.

"You see, my boy," Edward Thornton said to Nelson, "Thornton Enterprises has always experimented with revolutionary ideas in land development. Folks around here laughed at my father Adrian and old Chief Great Wind as they talked about rivers in the desert and living with the mountains and sky, as the Indians did. And now our plans for retirement condominiums seem like wild schemes, but, mark my words, they will be built. That is where you come in. I need to slow down, but Helen knows this business well, and she needs a good dependable man like you to keep her from running with her wild ideas."

Lundy listened to the laughter, but somehow it wasn't the same kind he heard from Nora and Big Lund, where hearts were light like warm sunshine. There was an edge to this laughter that Lundy didn't understand, and he turned his attention away from the partiers and toward his new friends.

Tomanto was busy preparing the steaks for the grill. The charcoal fires were just right and Teena had hot oil ready to dip French fries. A large wooden bowl filled with salad greens and vegetables sat on a nearby table.

Tomanto pointed to the sky, "Look, Lundy-Boy, drink in all the beauty of the sky and mountains. This valley will become a part of you. The mountains will seem like old friends. Some never see the beauty of the evening, but this is when a wise person refreshes his soul before going to bed. Someday I will tell you stories about the valley and the mountains.

Helen's voice interrupted, "Kips, I don't know much about children, but don't you think *that child* should go to bed?"

No one had noticed Lundy until then when suddenly everyone seemed to think he should be in bed. There had been a time change, they said, and it really was very late, even though it was barely dark. But he didn't want to go to bed all alone in that big room, without his stuffed animal friends, without Nora's prayers.

Kips quickly answered Helen, "Teena has prepared Lundy's supper and we will put him to bed when everyone is served. At that moment Teena padded in softly, "Come, Little Chief, it is time for your steak and Teena's big French fries."

Teena spoke softly, "I think I'll call you Chief Little Wind, after Tomanto's grandfather. Someday Tomanto will tell you about his grandfather."

Lundy went inside with Teena but heard the laughter on the patio and saw the steaks Mr. Thornton said no one could grill as well as Tomanto. Meggie was serving the family on the patio so Teena stayed with Lundy, who ate quickly, and then she took him upstairs to his room. Teena ran a tub of warm water and when Lundy had bathed and climbed into his pajamas Teena crooned an old Indian song. He'd only been there a minute when Lundy suddenly remembered the clock he'd snuck into his suitcase and he wouldn't settle down until he'd found it — and his blanket. "Nora gave this clock to me and I must wind it every night because it says, Ì love you,' over and over." He brought the clock to Teena and asked her to set it. She placed it beside Lundy's bed. Later, as she lovingly tucked him in, she heard a step behind her — Nels had come to say good-night to his son.

"Thank you, Teena, for helping Lundy. Now I'll hear his prayers and tuck him in. This has been a long day..." he added quietly.

Teena smiled and padded quietly down the stairs. Under her breath she added, "And say a prayer for yourself, Mr. Lundstrom. You will have many long days ahead. Good-night Chief Little Wind," she murmured to herself.

eleven

The
Sound of Hope

The cold wind of February, 1966, blew through the pampas grass. Nora's garden, covered with leaves, waited to be turned for spring planting. The trees lifted bare arms to the gray skies where lonely seagulls cried in the wind. Inside the house, Nora rocked quietly while Big Lund put another log on the fire. The silence and loneliness in the big house seemed overpowering, uninvited, unwelcomed.

Miss Lottie's cane sounded on the sidewalk while King barked a welcome. Missy and King found a sheltered place and stretched out to rest, both too old and too tired to romp.

Big Lund hung Miss Lottie's coat near the fireplace and she took her place beside Nora. "Been meaning to bring over these angel trumpet seeds since fall. Planting time comes before you know it. Winter seems longer this year, but then it always does. Good for the ground to rest."

Nora poured coffee. Miss Lottie continued, "No, Big Lund, don't go. I come with no woman talk today. God knows I got little enough time to say what I've been hankering to say. Some things need saying before it gets too late.

"I'll be ninety next month and those younguns of mine been fixing and fussing around like I don't know they're planning a big to-do."

Miss Lottie chuckled. "Didn't we have a fine party for our sixtieth anniversary? Old Jake loved every minute of it — gone now — oh Lordy, how I do miss my Jake. But then I'll be going soon and I'll see him again. Life's like that — winter time and then comes the spring.

"Sometimes I just ramble on, but I really come to tell you just how much folks on the sound here love you both. We all be grieving mighty hard that you haven't heard from Nelson."

Nora leaned forward, defensively.

"No, Nora, just wait. I know you don't want to talk about it, but I'm here to tell you that some things need talking out. It's been nineteen months since Nels took Lundy-Boy away. I've been studying mighty hard about this. Sometimes I believe what I can't see more than what I see.

"I know it all looks mighty hateful — kinfolk cutting themselves away, like cutting a boat from shore. Been pondering long and hard, and come to see fear instead of hate.

"I felt mighty uneasy when everything went so fast — eloping and all. I remember how thankful you were to see Nelson so happy. Old Missy didn't cotton to it though; she growled every time. She did!

"Just maybe Helen felt something here — maybe God — and maybe she was afraid of what she felt or of anything that could take Nelson away from her. She had to own him — as she probably owned everything she ever wanted."

Nora sat back.

"Then again, I see fear in Nelson — fear of the old memories, Melissa's house, the grave — and fear of the old numbness of grief that paralyzed him. Helen made him alive again.

"Now mind you, what they are doing is wrong, mighty, powerful wrong — cutting themselves off from their folks and all; but we do wrong if we don't put them in God's hands.

69

"I know I ramble, but hear me out. I don't mean no harm, but you cut yourselves off in the winter of grieving, just like Nels did. Grief is a lonely place and one can't stay there too long. Spring follows winter and time to plant comes after the cold."

Big Lund added a log to the fire and tried to hide a tear on his cheek. Nora reached for the coffee pot and just let her tears flow freely. They were silent as the logs crackled in the fireplace.

Finally, Nora spoke. "I keep reliving the wonderful days Melissa's, the baby, the new house, Christmas, and all the good times with Melissa's folks — all of us together. We were one big family. Then the accident. Nels changed. The Newtons left but we still had Lundy."

Big Lund spoke up, his voice husky with emotion. "Lundy followed me all over. When Helen said how much better off Lundy would be — education and travel — and implied that we were too old, well, I thought maybe it was best for him to be with young parents. I just never dreamed they wouldn't visit or invite us to Arizona. And I haven't tried to force any meeting. I thought perhaps Nels was ashamed of us and I didn't want to make life difficult for him or Lundy.

"It's been hard on Mike and Wilma too," Lund admitted, and continued, "Chad flew out to Arizona, but the secretary said that Helen and Nelson were in Europe on business. Chad said the house was a mansion — two houses. One for the Thorntons and one for the Lundstroms. There was a swimming pool and tennis courts. Lundy was with his tutor attending a horse show, so Chad didn't get to see anyone. He left a message with his hotel number, but no one called back. Nelson's telephone number is unlisted, so it's difficult to reach him except through the secretary at the office."

Nora interrupted and Lottie heard the bitterness in her tone, "We've tried everything. The packages, even the letters, are returned. How could Helen have fooled us? How can Nels forget his own people? What will happen to Lundy?"

"Heard tell a sermon on thoughts, Nora," Miss Lottie said, nudging her way back into the conversation. "The preacher said the mind was like a tree and thoughts like branches. Those thoughts get all tangled up in each other and will move any which way the wind blows. We have to get down to the root and grow new branches — new thoughts. The psalmist said, 'In the multitude of my thoughts God comforts me.' God brings new life, new strength to the root. He brings new thoughts, and the Good Book says, 'Whatsoever things are true and lovely — think on these things.' Then our thoughts don't get tangled up in the past and present and fear of the future. You missed a good sermon, Nora and Big Lund, and that brings me to what I really came to talk about.

"You have been cutting yourself off from church — just where you needed to be. That's where your friends are and, more than that, you've been missing some powerful preaching. Dr. Park's preaching been mighty good. He knows his time is short and seems like he wants to tell his flock all he can.

"Don't mean no harm, but sometimes folks run away from God in grief, when they should be running to Him.

"When Melissa died it was your faith that sustained folks all around. Remember how folks came to you for help and prayer when they suffered grief and loss? Now, Nelson and Lundy aren't here — like a living death, but I'm here to tell you to get back into the church where other folks can help you. Put Nelson, Lundy, and Helen into God's hands. No telling what He can do. In the meantime, we must stand strong. God never gets folks out of the storm until He gets the storm out of folks."

Big Lund looked away.

"The Bible says to keep ourselves in the love of God," Miss Lottie added. "When we pray for Nelson, Lundy, and Helen, we have to stand and forgive. We might not understand, but we must forgive. Only then can God hear our prayers."

Big Lund walked over to Nora and drew her close. "Nora-Girl, Miss Lottie's right. We have locked out the world while we locked ourselves into grief, wondering what we did wrong and how we could have prevented it. It's time to lay our burden down, and reach out. Grief is selfish sometimes." He turned to their friend. "Miss Lottie, we love you. I know you love us, and, believe me, we'll be back in church. May God forgive us for our blindness."

Miss Lottie tapped her cane delightedly. "I knew it! I knew it! You'll be coming back stronger in faith than ever before."

After she'd had two cups of coffee, Miss Lottie mentioned the one other concern she'd meant to bring up. "By the way, what did Nelson do with his house? Been standing empty these years, and that's not good — even with the painting and fixing."

Nora was able to laugh at Miss Lottie's question. "Helen made fun of the house, called it 'quaint.' Lundy hid in it and almost made them miss their plane."

"That's my boy, Nora. I'm telling you that child is coming home. I get that knowing feeling in my soul. You better pray and be looking for that boy. Now about the house?"

"We could tell Nelson was hurt when Helen called it quaint and suggested he sell it. He wouldn't do that, but he did turn it over to Lundy — and Big Lund until Lundy was of age. After all, it was a wedding gift."

"I'll tell you one thing, that Lundy-Boy is like Big Lund. He had more sense than grown folks. Like I tell you, I got that knowing in my soul. Lundy is coming home someday. He used to sit on my porch and talk like a grown man. Yes sir, they'll be coming home. The ocean, the house, Big Lund and you, Nora — those are ropes pulling them to home."

Lottie continued. "By the way, I know the new young preacher and his wife are looking for a house near the beach. Since our own Dr. Parks is retiring, we need to get this young preacher settled. They have a little girl and a boy about nine years old — like Lundy. Might be nice to have children close by. Not many children here, you know. The house is in your name and all — not good to be empty, Nora."

"We'll talk it over, Miss Lottie," Big Lund promised.

"Well, time to pick up my feet and get to home. I rightly don't need this cane, but the younguns said it could be tolerable handy to shoo the dogs. They don't fool me none — think I'm old, do they?

"Don't forget what I said, Nora, and do come sit a spell in my parlor. I keep a good fire. Mighty cool of an evening when the wind comes up. I've missed you."

Nora wrapped her arms around her old friend and kissed her cheek, wrinkled like oak bark from the wind. "Oh, dear friend, you are never old, just ageless in wisdom. We'll think about the house for the new preacher. It's time to throw off the garments of heaviness and put on the garment of praise for what we have. I know I'll see Lundy again. Nelson will come home. Like you, I have that 'knowing' in my heart."

Big Lund wrapped his arms around the two women. They felt his strength. "Miss Lottie, I think you can send that preacher over here. We'll take a look at the house together. We need to do something for someone else again. Now is a time for giving. Let's do it, Nora-Girl; let's just open Melissa's house to the new preacher."

Miss Lottie moved steadily down the road tapping her cane to keep time with her singing, "Some bright morning — I'll fly away."

Big Lund watched her go down the road, then turned to put a log on the fire.

"Nora-Girl, let's call Wilma and Mike and tell them about the house, and let them know that this is the day the Lord has made and we are going to rejoice in it. Perhaps they can come for a visit."

Suddenly the Big House was alive again, the crackling logs blending with the sound of laughter, the sound of hope.

twelve

Big Lund

T he two Lundstrom homes at the beach were divided by a large lot. From the upstairs windows in the Big House, Lund watched the rolling ocean on one side and the sound, with his boat tied to the pier, on the other side. Often this snug corner of the house missed the violence of the storms.

Lund stared across the way at Nelson's house, empty since Melissa's death. Miss Lottie's suggestion about a home for the preacher stirred a desire in Big Lund to open the house for the new family. It would be good, Lund mused, to hear the sounds of life again. Tomorrow he would check for repairs; tomorrow the preacher's wife could select the paint for the empty rooms.

That decided, Big Lund sat back in the porch chair and put his feet on the railing. Shrimp boats were heading home in the sunset, much as his grandfather's sailing ship had made its way over the waters toward Norway.

Karl Lundstrom, Big Lund's father, was only fifteen when he left his home in Norway to work as a carpenter in his uncle's shop in New York. Years later, he formed his own company which grew into a prosperous construction firm. Like Big Lund, Karl Lundstrom was a strong, independent, hard-working Norwegian.

When he was young, he was sure he would never marry. Succeeding in his business in America was all he cared about — until he met Karen Engstrom, the minister's daughter, who had a Nordic beauty of her own and a fierce love for reading. Immediately Karl began attending church, not to hear the sermon, but to watch Karen sing in the choir. Eventually he mustered enough courage to forget his Norwegian accent and invite the vivacious Karen to go for a ride on the Staten Island ferry.

Karen's laughter and humorous stories of parsonage life disarmed Karl and, to his surprise, he poured out all his dreams to her. Karen soon realized the depth of character and integrity in this quiet, young man. A deep love grew between them and the day came when their wedding was the talk of the Scandinavian community.

Into this Norwegian family Big Lund was the firstborn, then Mark and his two sisters, Ingrid and Liza. Karl, who had become a devout Christian, read the Bible to his family and, in turn, each member shared the father's faith in Jesus Christ.

Over the years the Lundstrom name became a household word among the immigrants as an example of the success that was available in the new world. Karl took his family to Norway to visit the old homeplace and see the churchyard where his parents were buried. "Children, never forget the rock you vere hewn from," he reminded them often.

Big Lund was remembering the rock from which he was hewn. He missed his parents, for part of the rock was missing. He felt a lump in his throat when he remembered leaving his father's house in New York. It all came back too clearly:

"Ja, I vork hard to build a good company. I need you, Lund, but a man has to do vot he has to do. The girl and the ocean? Two good reasons. Ja? The main reason is to do God's vill. Don't forget that, my son. No other reason comes before the vill of God. That goes for me, too. Since you have prayed, and believe God's vants you to build on the North Carolina coast, then you must. That comes before my vant to keep you in the family business. Ja, ve are builders, you and I. Mark is the business man. But you and I like to build vith our hands."

Big Lund looked over the ocean, remembering how he met Robert Johnson, a Navy man from North Carolina. Later he visited the coast and met Leonora, Robert's sister. Their love grew, until he knew he wanted to be with her forever and the lure of the ocean drew him to the North Carolina shore. He remembered his father's parting words:

"You and Robert Johnson should make a good team. He likes the business part and you like to build. I am thankful that he is a Christian. 'Be not unequally yoked together with unbelievers' goes for the home and the business. God's order never changes. Ja, enough talk about business. Never forget your home, Lund."

Big Lund could almost see his father shaking his long finger at him. "Never cause your mama vun minute of grief. A man can hurt many people in his life, but if he grieves the heart of his mama, there is little hope for home. Oh, ja, sometimes you argue with your papa, but you never talked back to your mama. That's ven I took the strap! Ja, and if you don't write or come to see her, I vill still take the strap."

Big Lund rocked quietly on the porch. The years were rolling before him like the waves of the ocean. His parents were gone now. He could almost feel his father's arms around him. "So foolish I talk to such a good boy. Never did you cause us pain. God be vith you and the beautiful Leonora. I just can't stand to see my Karen cry."

Big Lund remembered how he held his beautiful mother, her golden hair sprinkled with gray. "Mother, I will come soon. It is something I have to do. I love the stretch of sand, and endless rolling ocean; the warm wind in the pines, the sunshine and gardens. Besides you are all coming for the wedding."

Big Lund rocked quietly on the porch. Once again he felt the sadness of saying good-bye, as the train left New York. A tearful family had waved to him. "You can't go home again" seemed to settle over him like a cloud.

Then came the happy memories of his parents' visit to meet Leonora and her family. Karen loved Leonora and the two shared family traditions — with Leonora promising to observe a traditional Norwegian Christmas Eve, even with Jule Kake. After the beautiful wedding in the Community Church, Lund brought his young bride to the house on the sound.

When baby Nelson was born, Karen held her grandson in her arms and crooned a Norwegian lullaby. Karl Lundstrom beamed with pride: "Ja, he's another builder." Nelson had met the "rock" from which he, too, was hewn. For that, Big Lund was thankful.

From the porch he could see Nora wipe her hands on her apron and put the garden vegetables in her basket. She slipped out of her gardening shoes. He heard her stirring about in the kitchen. The shrimp boats were coming home. Suddenly Big Lund felt deep choking sobs, "Nelson, Nelson! Oh my God, how can my son forget his home? My son, my son, you even took the most precious gift in the world, our grandson Lundy-Boy. Surely the wind will carry our love across the miles — then you will know how you have broken our hearts."

As Big Lund watched the boats turn homeward, he thought, *Everything turns homeward. When night comes, everyone wants to go home. Even Papa Karl took one last trip to Norway before he was buried in New York.* Something stirred in Big Lund. He wanted to go Home. The faces of his mother and father and gentle Melissa came before him like a preview of the gathering. The tightness in his chest wouldn't leave.

"Big Lund," Nora called softly, "you have been in another world. I called you for supper but you didn't answer me." Nora pulled up a chair beside him and they rocked together. She leaned over and put her face against his. "They will come home, Big Lund. They will come home."

Big Lund was sure they would but he wondered whether he'd be there to greet them. He was tired of repairing old homes by himself. "Dreams come and go, Nora-Girl, but love for each other and the family is in the heart from God." He squeezed her hand. "Nora, you are the only girl

I ever loved. If I should go before you, always remember that I will be close. The beach house is our home — it's all ours: the salt spray, the rolling waves, the sunsets and the shrimp boats coming home. Our Nelson and Lundy-Boy will come home someday."

The chest pain was gone now. Big Lund stood, pulling Nora up beside him. "Come," he said, "Let's eat our supper and then go for our walk on the beach."

But late that night, Nora remembered that Big Lund walked a little slower and held her hand a little tighter. She fell asleep with the wind crying in the pines.

thirteen

The Birthday Party

I was December 5, 1966.

Lundy jumped out of bed. This was his birthday! He was nine years old, and for a moment he was in North Carolina, dreaming of Nora's cake and candles. Then he remembered — there would be no party. Helen and his father had gone on a business trip for the Thornton Enterprises and wouldn't return until Sunday. They'd left big gifts with fancy wrappings and bows with Teena and Kips. There was no school so Lundy could play all day. But he felt alone. He dressed quietly and went into the kitchen.

"Happy Birthday, young man." With a mock bow Kips invited Lundy to Teena's breakfast of sausage and pancakes. "Looks like we'll have a party by ourselves. Besides I have a surprise for you — but only after you eat."

Kips's laughter made Lundy feel better. They ate together in the cheerful breakfast room, and later they would go to the sun porch to open the gifts.

Long ago Lundy had learned to avoid Meggie, the house maid, who barely hid her hostility toward Lundy. "Children

79

should be seen and not heard," she often quoted. Whatever Helen asked Meggie did. No questions asked. When Helen said she was to get all of the mail — no exceptions — Meggie understood.

Although he had not heard from Nora and Big Lund in two-and-a-half years, Lundy continued to ask about mail, and especially on his birthday. He was alone in the yard when the red, white, and blue mail car drove up to the box. Meggie was on the phone, taking orders from Helen. Lundy ran to greet the mailman. "It's my birthday," he exclaimed. "Is there anything for me?"

"Well, now here's a package addressed to Lundy Lundstrom. Could that be you, young man?"

"Yes, that's me," Lundy exclaimed. "You must be new. The other mailman never had anything for me."

"This is my first day, young fellow. The old mailman moved away. Perhaps I'll bring more surprises to you." Then he was gone.

Clutching the package, Lundy ran to his room. He didn't want anyone to touch his treasure, not even Kips. Lundy closed the door and tore off the brown wrapping and then the gift wrap. There in the folds of tissue paper was the gift from Noragram and Big Lund — a large sailing boat. Lundy danced around the room. It was just like one of the boats docked at Wrightsville Beach. Like the boat Big Lund took him sailing on.

When Kips found Lundy and heard the story about the new mailman, a dark scowl crossed his face. What he'd suspected for many months must be true: Miss Helen and Meggie were in a conspiracy to keep any mail from Lundy. *Did Nelson know?* Kips wondered. *Or had Helen spirited Nelson's letters away as well?*

As if to clean Lundy's room, Kips scooped the brown wrapping from the floor, searching for an address. Now he could write to Lundy's grandparents, but that would come later. Today he had a birthday surprise for this young lad who had brought so much happiness into his life. He slipped his arm lovingly around Lundy's shoulders, admiring the sailboat in the boy's hand. Finally, he said, "We must go to the east patio where the sun shines over the mountains to bless a new day. Teena has a surprise for you."

When Lundy saw Teena, he called out, "Look, Teena, my grandparents didn't forget me this year." Lundy held up his shiny new sailing ship. "And I'll never forget them." As if to himself, he added, "No one will ever take this ship away, even if I'm one hundred years old."

Kips laughed his approval and shot a knowing look to Teena. He was certain the boy referred to his fear of Helen taking his boat away. They would need wisdom to outwit Meggie and Miss Helen.

"I thought you'd like to join our party," Teena said sweetly when Meggie walked into the room. "Master Lund is nine years old today. Show Meggie your boat, Lundy." Teena watched silently.

Reluctantly Lundy held up the gift.

"Where did you get that?" Meggie snapped, her thin lips taut, her face wrinkled with bitterness.

"The postman brought it. It's from Noragram and Big Lund."

"Miss Helen gets the mail!" Meggie shouted. Quickly composing herself she added, "How nice. Now let's see what's in the other packages."

But Tomanto had seen what he wanted to know. Meggie would have to be watched. If possible, he would sometimes intercept the mailman at the foot of the driveway. And Miss Helen? He would have to tread softly around Miss Helen. The beautiful, spoiled, utterly charming Miss Helen had a compulsion to control people. But why the boy? What had the boy done? Had Teena been right all along?

Teena had long suspected Helen's devious nature but Tomanto deliberately covered her faults. He dared not admit that Helen would even destroy him if it served her purpose. Tomanto seemed to hear his grandfather's words, "Listen my child Tomanto, and let your words be few. A man is thought wise when he weighs his words."

"Yes, Great Wind, I will remember," Tomanto whispered. "I will be wise. Oh, Great Spirit of the forest, mountains and the valleys, come with the wisdom of Great Wind."

Finally, he turned his attention to Lundy's happiness. "Look, Meggie," Lundy was saying. "There are books and crayons and a game. And look at the art set that Kips and Teena gave me." He set up the small easel and held up the drawing paper and paints. "If Kips will help me, I'll paint a picture of the ocean for your room, Meggie."

Her stern face softened. "I think I'd like that, Master Lundy. Yes," she added, "I'd like that very much."

"Did you ever get neat gifts like this on your birthday, Meggie?"

She shook her head. "I never had a birthday party." When Lundy frowned, she tried to explain, "You see, I lived with an austere aunt who thought that birthday parties were...were nonsense." Bitterness squeezed her words.

"Aren't you glad you missed the mailman this morning, Meggie?" Kips asked. "You would have missed the boy's joy."

Meggie looked away.

Lundy was unwrapping his biggest gift. "It's from Dad and Helen," Lundy announced. Then a look of surprise came into his face as he lifted another beautiful sailboat from the package. He read the card out loud: *Have fun sailing this in the swimming pool. Dad.*

The sailing ship was bigger and better than the one from Noragram and Big Lund. Lundy's eyes went to the smaller boat; he was puzzled. He held the two boats up for everyone to see. "Big Lund took me sailing and fishing sometimes — like he used to take my father. But after my mother died, my dad wouldn't go out in the boat again. He kept saying that maybe if he hadn't gone fishing that day, maybe Mom wouldn't have died."

Kips understood that the gift of the sailboat from his father was a special memory from the past — something for Lundy to hold in his heart on those many occasions when his father was away on business trips with Helen. But Kips knew that the smaller boat from Noragram and Big Lund had touched the boy's heart more. Suddenly, to ease the boy's sadness, Kips exclaimed, "Now the surprise, Master Lundy! Teena and I are going to take you on a trip."

Lundy brightened.

"I already have your father's permission for us to go to the zoo. Teena packed a picnic lunch. How about that for a birthday party?"

Lundy scurried to his feet. "Would you like to go with us, Meggie?" he asked.

"To a birthday party, Master Lundy?"

"Yes."

She almost smiled. "I've never been to a birthday party. Never had one of my own. I only wish I could go with you." Her gruff voice was unusually gentle.

* * *

As the black Cadillac moved easily over the highway, Tomanto told story after story about the Arizona countryside. Lundy listened politely, but he kept running his fingers over the bow of the sailing ship from Noragram and Big Lund.

When they reached Papago Park, Tomanto persuaded Lundy to leave the boat safely in the car. All afternoon Lundy led the procession from pen to pen, field to field — stretching his neck like Freckles the giraffe; making faces at Hazel, the gorilla; devouring peanuts and cotton candy.

Finally, Teena opened the basket on the picnic lawn away from the animal cages. She spread a red and white checkered cloth on the ground. Blue mugs and matching tin plates came out of the magical basket and held endless surprises: fried chicken, potato chips, cantaloupe, peaches and ham biscuits. A jug of lemonade and a tin of chocolate chip cookies completed the feast.

All too soon, the day ended and three tired people headed home. The Arizona sky was ablaze with a colorful sunset that quickly turned to darkness. As the moon shone overhead, Lundy fell asleep.

"Dream on, little friend," Kips said.

"About what?" Teena asked.

"About sailing ships and his old home on Wrightsville Beach."

Teena stroked Lundy's head tenderly and spoke softly to Tomanto. "This is a strange child, too old to be so young. I would like to have known his mother and grandparents. Mr. Nelson doesn't know his own child. It must be the Great Spirit who brought this child to us. Miss Helen would destroy him and you are wiser than she. You are such a good father, so wise and patient. If only I could have given you a son."

Kips reached out to touch the work-worn hand, "Teena you have given me more than a man could wish for. The dream of our own son is past, but now, in our old age, we have been given a child. Great Wind would say, Be thankful for what is in your hand.' We must not let Miss Helen send him to boarding school ever. I will talk to Mr. Nelson again this fall just like I did when the child refused to move out of his room into the new house Mr. Thornton built for Helen."

It was Mr. Thornton who reminded Helen and Lund that their social and political obligations kept them traveling most of the time. "Lundy would be more at home in his own room, with Kips and Teena taking him to school and assisting with the spelling and reading." That settled the issue. At least for the present, Lundy was still safe in their care.

Kips added softly, "The Great Spirit willed it, Teena."

Late into the night Kips watched the star-filled sky, like a canopy over the sleeping household. Then he reached for his pen and hurriedly wrote a letter and addressed it to: Mr. and Mrs. Lund Lundstrom, Wrightsville Beach, North Carolina.

fourteen

A Time
For Choosing

A large driveway separated the two homes on the Thornton Estate. Lundy rode his bicycle back and forth across the expanse of pavement. Although he was free to go in and out of both houses, he stayed closer to the Thornton residence and his beloved Kips.

The Sunday after Lundy's birthday, Helen and Nelson were finally home, ready for a morning swim with Lundy. "Look what the new mailman brought, Dad," Lundy said, holding up the gift from his grandparents. "It's from Noragram and Big Lund. They didn't forget."

Nels scowled. "It's almost like the one I gave you." He scrutinized the vessel, his neck pulsating. "Why now? Why this year after ignoring us for so long?"

Helen stepped between Nels and Lundy. "Where did you get this, Lundy?" she demanded.

Meggie cowered in the doorway as Helen turned to Nelson. "If it's like the one we gave him, he doesn't need both of them. We'll get rid of the one from his grandparents." Her eyes were cold, angry.

Kips saw the defiance in Lundy's face, the fear on Meggie's, and the questioning look in Mr. Nelson's eyes. "Here, Miss Helen," Kips offered, "I'll take care of it."

She grabbed the boat from Nels and thrust it into Kips' broad hand. "Make certain you do," she told him. Then as usual, she turned the conversation, asking with animated expression about the other gifts.

Lundy stood barefoot in his new swim suit. He was trembling as he leaned against his dad. "Thank you for the boat you gave me, Dad," he said quietly. "We can sail it in the swimming pool now if you'd like." Then edging even closer, he whispered, "But I want my other boat, too. The one Noragram sent. I'll keep it in my room."

Nelson nodded, then stole a glance at Helen. "You go ahead, Son," he said. "I'll watch you sail the boat from here." His voice was empty, toneless.

The toy boat seemed to bring it all back again, especially as he watched his son sail it. Tomanto had attached a long string to the stern and Lundy let it go out to the center of the pool. But the picture blurred — Nels kept seeing Wrightsville Beach and his dad's ship bobbing on the water. Melissa was there. Melissa! There was always Melissa. Warm, gentle, loving Melissa. Some part of him had died when she died. Only Helen had made him forget, but not completely — at least not today.

Helen had awakened his manhood and his drive for power. As he thought of his father, Big Lund, he viewed him as a good, dependable rock, always there, but when he met the Thorntons, he saw the challenge of adventure for high stakes. From then on, Nels had focused on one goal — power.

He had felt powerless after Melissa's death, powerless to rear his own son. As a Navy pilot, he had wanted to die, but even death eluded him there. Then Helen came. Helen had come with her beauty, tantalizing every fiber of his being. When he was with her, he was beyond the reach of pain. He could defy the past, and drink the passion of the present, the power of the future.

Nelson had cut the moorings to his past, and to prove his worth to the Thornton Enterprises, he'd driven himself relentlessly. Edward Thornton had recognized Nelson's ability and continually turned over more responsibility to him. More power.

The swirling social life had added glamour and prestige. Nelson was the envy of every man when he walked into a crowded room with the dazzling Helen on his arm. And, although he knew he should be a better father, he had Lundy near him. Wasn't that ample? Didn't he — Nelson Lundstrom — have everything a man could hope for? So why was he restless? Where was his peace? Why did a sailboat floating in the swimming pool make old memories roll in like the waves on Wrightsville Beach? Nelson stretched uneasily in the lounge chair. He saw Lundy wave at him but his eyes went beyond Lundy to Helen on the diving board.

She was wearing her sleek black swim suit, her long dark hair flowing freely. She smiled at Nelson temptingly, then dove into the water and moved gracefully, with long even strokes, up and back the length of the pool. At the sight of her, Nelson's blood quickened and he jumped into the water, challenging her to see if she could out swim him, challenging her so the haunting memories of home and Melissa would go away.

With a steady but swift tug, Lundy pulled his sailboat to "shore," afraid that the waves from their splashing might capsize his treasure.

* * *

Late that night Helen and Nelson unlocked the door to their home, returning after a black tie dinner with the new senator and his wife. Nelson stood and watched the stars in the clear sky before pulling the drapes on the night and following Helen upstairs.

In their bedroom, glass doors opened to a balcony where Helen stood in a shimmering silver blue gown, her black hair brushed into loose curls. Every time he saw her outlined against a moonlit sky he tensed with excitement. He longed for them to have a child.

Gently Helen helped him out of his shirt and suit. To tease him she kept slipping just out of his reach, until she turned her warm sensual body to his outstretched arms.

Later she murmured contentedly, "Please don't talk of children. I only want you."

Holding her close, with her warm mouth against his, Nelson quietly agreed. Nora and Big Lund faded into the distance, like a ship beyond the horizon. Helen pressed closer.

When Helen was asleep, Nelson sought her again. Why was he never at peace? The hunger in him was never satisfied, yet Helen's passion matched his own. Helen stirred beside him and sensed his tension. An overpowering desire to quench the thirst within him made Nelson draw Helen's sensuality into his and they moved together on a wave of passion — beyond the pain within his soul.

Helen smiled to herself, assured she had Nelson firmly in her power, then she fell asleep again. Nelson floated out to sea in his dreams, and there just beyond his reach, was gentle Melissa and Lundy-Boy. In the distance the small boat was drifting out to sea, its rope cut from the moorings.

fifteen

The Letters

Big Lund sorted through the mail, then stopped — startled. The big envelope in the unfamiliar handwriting was postmarked Arizona. He was trembling as he tore the envelope open.

Tears were coursing down his cheeks as he rushed into the house, crying, "Nora-Girl . . . Miss Lottie. There's a letter from our Lundy."

Big Lund clutched the New Year's Day card and the letters as he waited for Nora to wipe her hands on her apron. "Hurry, woman, hurry," he pled.

As soon as Nora took her place at the large oak table, he sat down beside her. He pushed the tray with the three coffee mugs to the middle of the table. The cinnamon toast was cold.

Across the table from them, Miss Lottie thumped her cane on the polished hardwood floor. She leaned toward Lund. "It's good news. I've got that knowing in my bones."

Lund nodded through his tears.

"I've been telling you two to expect miracles. Can't see what you're waitin' for, boy. Unfold that letter and read it."

Still Lund hesitated.

Miss Lottie tapped her cane impatiently. "Lord, have mercy. I wouldn't miss this letter for anything. Heard from the postal clerk that something special was coming to your place. Folks in the sound about to die of curiosity by now. Me, too. That's why I plumb got to walking over here early today." Miss Lottie slapped her knee delightedly and reached down to pat Missy. "Hurry, Lund. Hurry."

Nora watched Big Lund spread the letter on the table. Then he read, his voice choked with emotion: "I promised to send this letter from your grandson Lundy. He wanted to thank you for his birthday present."

Tears trickled down Nora's cheek as she peeked over Lund's shoulder and read the childish scrawl:

Dear Noragram and Big Lund.
I miss you very much. Thank you for my boat. I went to the zoo and had a picnic. Teena baked a cake. Daddy gave me a sailboat, too. Kips put a rope on it to sail in the swimming pool. But I like your boat best. I miss King, Miss Lottie, and Missy. I love you Noragram. I love you Big Lund. Someday I will come home. Kips is helping me with my spelling. Daddy is gone most of the time. I never get any letters. I just got my birthday card from the new mailman. I want Kips and Teena to come home with me. I love you.

Lundy-Boy   xOxOxOxO

Tears streamed down Nora's cheeks.

Miss Lottie thumped her cane. "Glory be!" she shouted. "I done told you about the knowing. That child's coming home someday. Don't go crying now, Nora. Big Lund, read that other letter."

Big Lund took Tomanto's letter and read:

I want you to know that Lundy is a fine boy and doing well. Teena and I are old servants on the Thornton estate. Mr. Nelson is a fine man and doing well in the family business. I have known Miss Helen since she was a baby and she loves your son very much. They make a handsome couple and are very busy.

I was taught by my wise old Indian grandfather, so I can see and understand many things. When I discovered that the mail was censured, I knew I could not remain silent. By accident Lundy received his birthday package and card. Nothing could have pleased him more.

Teena and I have no children. We love your grandson like our own child. Be assured that we will watch over him and I know that he will return to you someday.

It is most difficult to write this word of caution, for I have a deep sense of loyalty to the Thorntons. Miss Helen blinds the eyes of those who love her, so they cannot see her drive for power. I am also her faithful servant, but our love for Lundy made us write to you.

Please do not write to me. It would cause great grief for all of us. For Lundy's sake Teena and I must keep our role as his guardian. We can only do this as we keep our role as faithful household servants.

Be very careful how you write for Mr. Nelson's eyes are blinded by his passion for Miss Helen.

Even a lifetime of devotion to Miss Helen and her family would not keep me here if she knew of this letter. We would be dismissed without references, and Lundy would be sent to boarding school. Please understand this.

We promise to look after your grandson.

Faithfully,
Tomanto Tellentra

Big Lund, Nora and Miss Lottie sat quietly. Nora fingered Lundy's letter while the tears fell. "More than two-and-a-half years we waited!

Big Lund seemed weary. "The child is well," he added softly, "and my son is prosperous." Lund's shoulders drooped a little. "But is Miss Helen so powerful that a son can forget his home?" he asked wistfully.

Miss Lottie tapped her cane. "You only knew good women in your day, Big Lund. Your mother and sisters — all loving, generous, giving womenfolk. Then Nora here — only her man and his good counted for her."

Big Lund patted Nora's hand gently. "I know Miss Lottie, I know, but Nelson had his mother — and Melissa."

Miss Lottie's cane scratched across the floor. "You men folk are mighty weak — come the tempting Delilah kind. Huh, take Eve, she done got a perfect man all mixed up about God's will and man's will, and they end up choosing a devil's lie. How about that — and Adam, a perfect man?" Miss Lottie pointed her finger at Lund. "Now what about the strongest? That Samson fellow, big and strong, and look what happened to him when he got his beautiful smart head in the lap of Delilah? He got his power cut in a hurry. What about David — chosen by God to be a king? Didn't he get himself in a heap of trouble watching Bathsheba take a bath? Lord have mercy, that poor man forgot all about God's laws and ends up breaking one after the other." Miss Lottie was on a roll. "Then there was Solomon, the wisest man who ever lived. Beautiful women turned his heart away from God."

Miss Lottie thumped her cane louder. "But one thing I have to say, they repented and God forgave them. One day Nelson will see that Miss Helen is Eve, Delilah and Bathsheba all rolled into one.

"Mark my words, there will come a day when he will wonder how she looked like golden honey in the soft moonlight. Truth can be a cruel mirror, Big Lund. But with the truth will come a cleansing for his soul and then a healing. He will come home, Big Lund. Your boy will come home. As for Lundy-Boy — oh, glory be!"

Miss Lottie slapped her knee in anticipation. "It's as good as seeing — this believing. I see things no one else sees, and this one thing I see like it is right here now. I see Lundy-Boy right beside you, Nora, and you two will be laughing again.

"Now we owe God a thank you for that letter, and don't tell folks too much. Just say that you heard from Lundy and he is fine."

"What is that P. S. in the corner?" Nora asked. Big Lund squinted. "Looks like it says, 'I go to the reservation twice a year and I will take Lundy along to see the displays of art. You can write a letter to me c/o the Postmaster. He will save it for me.'"

Miss Lottie spoke up again, "The way I see it, Nora, that is an open door to get a letter through. But the best line we have is the praying line. That goes straight to God. He sent that Indian to take care of our boy and the best we can do is to pray for him and Teena. I ask you, who gave that kind woman a loving in her heart for our boy?"

"As for Helen, she needs our forgiveness and prayers more than anyone. That hungering for that beautiful woman never going to fill the empty place in Nelson's life. That stormy kind of loving may be exciting, but it is like the restless ocean, rolling and rolling on the dunes — never satisfied. The love of a woman like Melissa is like a drink of cool, clear water in the desert of life. There comes with it a peace and calm, like a quiet lake. Then again when the sorrows and joys of life come heaping on you, it is God's everlasting love that keeps us safe in the storm.

"Oh glory be, Nora, one of these days I'll be going to my real home, and all these tears will be plumb forgot. Yup — the younguns planning a big party. They think ninety is old. Humph! Wait till I celebrate in heaven, *ten thousand years, bright shining as the sun.* Come, Missy, you and me better amble to home."

Miss Lottie moved down the road singing, "We've no less days to sing God's praise, than when we first begun."

Nora watched her friend with misty eyes. Big Lund chuckled softly, "She forgot to sing, I'll fly away.'" A soft whisper of a breeze blew through the pine trees. Looking into the sky, Nora added softly, "Thank You, Lord."

Big Lund sat with his head bowed, holding the letters in his hand. "Two-and-a-half years was a long time to wait. God bless you, Tomanto."

The wind picked up through the pines and clouds hid the sun for a moment. Glancing up, Big Lund looked into the darkening sky. "Wind picking up Nora, might be a storm coming."

sixteen

The Preacher

The ocean rolled in with a soft gray mist that sprayed gently over Craig Cranston as he walked the beach in the early morning. Craig, a lanky, sandy-haired man with an angular face and deep-set blue eyes had come to love the beach community at Wrightsville.

At the university, Craig had changed his major from engineering to theology. After that, his life fell into place, especially when he'd met Carolyn, whose spiritual depth seemed to reach beyond him. He loved her dearly, not only for her music and humor, but for the deep love of God he sensed in her. Although he finally obtained his degree in theology, he knew Carolyn had something he didn't.

The move to Wrightsville to pastor the small Community Church had been a good one. He couldn't remember when his wife had been so happy. She loved her new home — the Lundstrom's house. And the kids — lands, were they happy. Young Bert, named for his grandfather Albert Cranston, was always following Big Lund around like a shadow. And little Rebecca — for months they wondered if she'd ever learn to walk, what with Nora and Miss Lottie always having a lap available or wanting to rock her. Things had gone along well for the Cranstons ever since they came to Wrightsville — no problems at all. At least, not until last night.

Craig bent into the wind, catching his breath, as he passed the Mason Inlet. The black despair of last night engulfed him again. Though he brushed at his ears, it was as though he could still hear the rescue squad's piercing siren. And then the phone call from Miss Lottie. "Preacher, there's been a drowning at the inlet. Folks are needing you pretty bad."

Four teenagers, wading in the shallow water at dusk, had suddenly stepped into deeper water and the rip tide currents had swept them to sea.

A nearby fisherman and a lone jogger heard their cries. Together they dragged one of the girls to the sandbar. The two boys, both good swimmers, attempted to rescue Cindy, the other girl. But she struggled, dragging Tim, one of the boys into the undertow with her. Though exhausted, the fisherman and jogger managed to drag the other nearly unconscious boy to safety. But Cindy and Tim were gone.

Craig shivered, remembering. He had gone immediately, of course, but he felt helpless, useless, as he moved among the rescue squad, the police, the reporters, the curious tourists. Finally Craig stopped by the fisherman.

When he saw Craig, he sobbed. "Preacher, we had their hands." He moaned. "They just slipped out of reach."

The jogger, a young man from the community, kept staring into space. "It's a miracle we weren't all swept out to sea. May God help the families of those kids. Warning signs all over..."

It struck Craig then that it was his job to tell the families that God would help them. But he wanted to run. He wasn't sure he believed it himself. He had walked away, the fisherman's words calling in the wind, "It's all the same on the surface, but that undertow..."

Craig turned now, and walked back over the same sandy trail, away from the beach. He couldn't go home yet...face Carolyn . . . admit his fears. A man of God afraid?

He kept walking, aimlessly. Finally, he stopped and looked up. He was only a block from Miss Lottie's. When he walked up to her porch, it was as though she had been expecting him.

"Come sit a spell," she offered. "I already have us some coffee and hot buns."

"You were expecting me?"

"I'm always ready — if someone comes a'callin'."

He slumped down beside her and listened intently to her rocking chair creaking and groaning with the sea. A grim silence engulfed Craig. Miss Lottie seemed to understand. She waited, rocking, rocking.

Craig broke the silence when he rammed his fist into the arm of her chair, almost spilling her coffee. "It's so unfair. It's all so unfair," he cried out in fury. "Two beautiful young people gone like that — dead."

"Young man," she said softly, "we can send out our whys on the wings of the morning to the throne of God and wait a lifetime for an answer."

"But, Miss Lottie, I have to conduct a double funeral tomorrow. What can I say?" In a mocking, clerical voice he intoned, "Dearly beloved, we are gathered to see God's will — two dead young people — "

Miss Lottie whirled around in her rocker. "Preacher man, that is enough! Complain and cry to God all you got a hankering to do, but I get mighty troublesome in my spirit when you complain *about* God. Plenty times I ask questions, and get angry, but I learned a long time ago not to blame God almighty for things happening in the world. Meaning no disrespect, preacher. I reckon your thinking been taking a wrong turn for some time. Let's just sit real quiet and look at what the creator of heaven and earth gave us."

"I shouldn't even be a preacher, Miss Lottie. I have too many doubts."

"In my way of thinking, that is the first sign of the making of a preacher. Nothing wrong with doubts; it is rebellious unbelief that destroys man's soul. I reckon a heap of doubts marched around with a heap of questions might just end up with a heap of faith. All that learning in the seminary don't make no preacher, no sir! All that studying about people — that psychology; and all that studying about God — that theology, no sir, that don't make preachers. Seminary is good, preacher, but to study about folks without God's love don't seem tolerable. Studying about God seems powerful wrong when a man don't know Him. We begin at the beginning — that is God.

"Look at Moses, the great lawgiver, and how he spent forty years in the desert. I reckon he marched with doubts and questions. Even when he met God, he didn't want to obey. He said, 'I can't talk.' Lord have mercy, preacher, we've been hearing Moses talk ever since. Even Isaiah said, 'Woe is me, I am undone.' Remember Paul said, 'I am the least.'

"No preacher got the right to tell folks about God, until he knows God for himself. Jesus said, 'I am the way, the truth and the life. No man cometh unto the Father but by me!' He also said to become like a child. First you have to know you belong to Him."

Miss Lottie grew silent. A shadow crossed her face, then bewilderment. She hesitated, bowed her head then took a deep breath. Softly, as to a child, she reached over to touch Craig's hand. "Preacher, I don't mean no offense, but have you ever given your heart to Jesus Christ and asked Him to live in you? Have you ever accepted God's gift of salvation? You can't go higher before you kneel at the cross and believe Jesus died for you.

"God so loved us that He gave His son. Jesus so loved us that He gave us the Holy Spirit. Then the Word of God comes alive. Only then can you stand in the pulpit and have answers from God's Word. I'm mighty ignorant of the world's knowledge, but I know that the fear of the Lord is the beginning of wisdom. It is good to start at the beginning."

Craig leaned forward — his face in his hands.

"I've been talking long, preacher, but deep in my heart I got the knowing, that you'll get answers to your doubts if you take one step of faith. A king or a beggar has to come the same way. A great city preacher or a little girl like me from the tobacco fields has to come the same way, with a humble heart, a bowed head, and a bended knee. For that I have a knowing."

* * *

Craig sat tense, silent. Within him pride raised its ugly head. He felt rage and the cry of loneliness. He clenched his fist then bit his lip. Slowly into his darkness came a verse he had preached from but hadn't known: "For God so loved the world." But he kept hearing, "For God so loved Craig." *God loves me! God loves me!*

Doubts and questions — the lifeless bodies of Tim and Cindy — rolled over him like the ocean. *On the surface it looks the same.* He heard it over and over. Like many others he stood and opened the Bible, Sunday after Sunday. Book reports, character building, current events — phrases and then the benediction. It all looked the same on the surface. But did anyone know or care about the riptide currents of life — currents that pulled a man's soul out to sea?

He could hear Miss Lottie breathing beside him, short, raspy sounds.

Another verse came to mind. "For God sent not His son to condemn the world, but that all the world through Him might be saved."

Craig fell to his knees weeping like a child. "My God, forgive me. My life has been a sham. Cleanse me with the precious blood of Jesus, shed for me. Create in me a clean heart — to worship you, God, and serve you. Forgive my sins and fill me with your Holy Spirit."

Miss Lottie knelt beside her rocker and put her arm on Craig Cranston's shoulder. She had a knowing that this preacher would be a man of God, loved and respected by the community.

When Craig finally stood to leave, he held Miss Lottie's frail form gently in his arms and kissed her wet cheeks. "You are the wisest friend I have. Thank you for your faith and courage. Your honesty." With a sweep of his hand, he said, "Look, the gray mist is beginning to lift. I must go, dear friend, and meet with the families of Cindy and Tim. But first, I must tell my wife she has a brand new husband."

seventeen

Hearth of Fire

Carolyn Cranston moved about her new home quietly. Little Rebecca was asleep with a plush teddy bear in her arms — a gift from Nora and Big Lund — and her thumb and blanket in place. How quickly she had outgrown Lundy's cradle and graduated to a crib.

Carolyn sat down with her coffee cup and open Bible and read, "In all thy ways acknowledge Him, and He shall direct thy paths." It had been a year since the Cranstons had moved into the Lundstrom house. Bert followed Big Lund around like a puppy follows its mother. Rebecca had two extra "grandmothers" to rock her. What a beautiful year it had been!

But today, a dark cloud hung over the community, and an even greater darkness had settled in her husband's heart. Carolyn ached for Craig. Deep inside she knew what Craig needed, but his spiritual eyes were blind. She could only pray.

Last Sunday, fifteen-year-old Cindy, a vivacious redhead, had whispered to Carolyn, "I'm going to be a nurse, just like you." Several weeks before, Tim, an honor roll student, had told Craig, "I want to be a preacher." Now they were dead. Tomorrow would be the funeral.

She silently prayed, "Oh, God, work all this sorrow around for the good of Your people — and please, help Craig. Help him to really minister to this community. Especially now in this tragic loss."

Carolyn was sure it was God's will for them to be here. There was a peace in this house and in her heart. It was Craig who was always restless. She remembered how they had met in Atlanta at a church social. It was love at first sight for the popular associate minister and Carolyn, a nurse at Baptist Hospital. "A perfect match," everyone had said, and within a few months they were married. As a child Carolyn had accepted Jesus Christ, and the Bible had became her life's textbook.

When Craig — her first real love — captured her heart she determined to be the best minister's wife possible. Only later did she discover Craig's restlessness, and daily she determined to be the wife he needed and to trust God to open his eyes to his own inner needs.

Miss Lottie, Nora and Big Lund were like family now. How she loved them! Craig seemed to enjoy the practical Miss Lottie, and he often sat on her porch just to rock and visit.

Carolyn drew strength from Nora's quiet depth of faith and together they worked in the garden and talked — of the past, present, and future.

Carolyn hoped she would never have to leave this house — it was the first one she'd lived in that felt like home. Big Lund had allowed her to pick out the wallpaper and paint. He had polished the wide pine floors to a golden glow. Nora had given them Lundy's cradle for Rebecca, and Miss Lottie had insisted on giving them some wonderful antiques that had been stored in her attic.

"Lord have mercy, child," she'd said. "Aunt Hortense left a houseful of old furniture to me. My Jake said it was no account so he put it in the attic, rug and all. The preacher saw it and said it was right smart antiques. Ha! Shows how much I know. Then I got to thinking how my younguns might get to squabbling over them so when my Jake died

I said, 'Someday I'll get shed of the junk.'"

Carolyn smiled as she recalled Miss Lottie's delighted chuckle. "You'd be doing me a mighty big favor to get all those fancy antiques out of the attic — rug and all." Carolyn looked at the Karastan rug on the floor, the hand-crafted dining room set, and the poster bed in their room. She never dreamed that she would have such a home. The day might come when she would have to leave this house, but now she was thankful for it. Then aloud she prayed again, "Please, God, help Craig."

Moments later she heard him coming up the flower-flanked brick walkway. A responsive chord of joy stirred within her as she heard him whistling AMAZING GRACE.

eighteen

The Passing Years

In the spring of 1973, Teena and Tomanto stood beside the corral gate and watched the sun go down behind the mountains. "Our boy rides well, Teena," Tomanto said.

"He is no longer a boy, Tomanto. He is a young man. Fifteen already."

"He handles himself well," Tomanto admitted, "and look how he handles that horse. Desert Wind should make a good showing in Scottsdale next week." Tomanto's face shone with pride. He watched Lundy slip out of the saddle and stroke the mare's white face gently.

"I'll take her into the stable and give her a good rubdown," Lundy called. "Okay?"

Tomanto nodded. The boy and the horse blended as one.

It had been Tomanto's suggestion to Nelson that his son was ready for an Arabian mare of his own. "You buy it for him," Tomanto had urged, "and I will teach him to ride and care for it."

Lundy had been riding Desert Wind for two years now — ever since his thirteenth birthday. They were inseparable.

Tomanto often rode alongside on a spirited stallion, another special gift from Nelson Lundstrom for caring for Lundy. *Or,* thought Kips, *were you trying to make up for never being home — for always being away with Miss Helen and never with your son?*

Together, Indian and boy galloped through the valley, Lundy dreaming of breeding prize-winning Arabian horses, and Kips dreaming of painting them. Sometimes they rode slowly, and then Kips would speak of the past as part of his dream for the future.

"You are surrounded by wealth and power, Lundy, but you're strong enough to control it and not let it control you. You must take advantage of what it can accomplish, but you must control how that power will be used in your life.

"I, too, have great wealth, but it is of the spirit, an inheritance from my grandfather Great Wind. It is a hunger to learn, to create, to love deeply, and to give what has been given to me. At times I feel like a caged lion, roaring on the inside to be free. But greater wisdom tells me that we create our own cages, for our spirits are free. I wait for the Great Spirit's time. You, too, Lundy must wait."

For weeks all of Tomanto and Lundy's efforts were centered on preparing Lundy for the Scottsdale horse show — a secret they were keeping from Nelson and Helen. Tomanto dared not risk Helen forbidding the boy to enter the show. They had been in Europe again for several weeks but were due back in time for the annual rodeo.

For years now, ever since Lundy came to live with them, Helen and Nelson had turned over the responsibility of Lundy's care to Tomanto and Teena. They rarely asked questions. They assumed that if there were problems they would hear about them.

Teena and Tomanto walked back to their tiny cottage from the corral as the Arizona sun was going down. "I think Lundy is ready, my Teena. It is time to show him my secret room. He is old enough to understand. I have taught him enough of Great Wind's words that he will understand my dreams."

"Then this is the night you've been living for — when you can show Lundy your real life's work?"

Tomanto nodded.

Just as they reached the door to the cottage, Lundy charged up behind them. "I think I'll stay over with you again tonight," he said. "No use to go back to the house."

Teena smiled. "Your couch is always ready, my son. This is always your home." She moved slowly across the room. "You sleep here, my son. You can go back to the mansion when Tomanto goes in the morning."

"But before you dream, my friend, of Desert Wind and the rodeo, I have a dream of my own to show you," Tomanto announced.

Lundy stopped short, his eyes wide. "A dream, Kips? Tell me. Show me."

"After dinner, my friend. After dinner."

Tomanto said, "Every man has a dream, Lundy-Boy. You dream of horses. I . . . I of painting. But dreams can't grow in roots and thorns — only in ground that is plowed soft with love and forgiveness. Hate only destroys us — not the ones we hate. I know about hate — for the white man, for other Indian tribes, but Great Wind's dream was to build bridges so the hate would be destroyed. He told me about the differences between the customs of our people, the Hopi Indians, and the Navajos. The Hopi Indians congregated in stone pueblos on the edge of mesas in northern Arizona. The Navajos preferred to cluster in towns. Both tribes had their shrines, their strong family roots, and conflict began long, long ago. But Great Wind had a dream for a road and he kept saying, "Do not build on conflict, build on need." It's taken years, but now there is a council from both tribes that works on the hard issues. They agree that to help their people these things must be provided — jobs, education, and a road, a road that will mean a better life for both tribes. They call it the Turquoise Trail, and you and I will see that road — because Great Wind had a dream. The differences are still there, but nothing good is built on hate.

"Great Wind worked for the future, as did Miss Helen's grandfather. The two of them spent long evenings together, being of one spirit. Before old Mr. Thornton died he persuaded Teena and me to come and live here where I could read, study, and paint. He told Great Wind that I would keep my people's traditions alive for the future and part of Mr. Thornton's dream was for me to learn all I could about the art I loved.

"When Mr. Thornton died, I thought my dreams had died, for his son Edward saw me only as a servant. The father knew me as a child with a dream. Young Mr. Thornton only knew me as a man with a task. But even though I'd lost the older Mr. Thornton and then Great Wind, I hadn't really lost my dream.

"Teena and I remained faithful servants to the son and his wife, and then to beautiful Helen. But as I served, my soul cried to be free — free to pursue my dream. We worked and saved our money so I could buy my paints. Late at night I would keep practicing my style. As often as I could I studied in the library and visited museums. No, my dream never died, and tonight I'm ready to show it to you. You are old beyond your years. You have great wisdom. And I think you'll understand why my dream is so important."

Kips led the way up the narrow winding stairway and into the attic room. He turned around just in time to see the astonished look on Lundy's face.

Teena's padded footsteps had followed them, and her bright eyes glistened with pride.

"Kips," Lundy exclaimed, "I knew you liked to draw and paint, but these are like the ones you showed me in the museum last year. These are wonderful."

Lundy moved slowly from one painting to the other. "This must be Great Wind." The face of the old man held him — the deep lines, the wise eyes and then the gnarled hands. "This is exactly how I pictured your grandfather, Kips. You've made your people and their land come alive: the buffalo, the big horns, and, oh, Kips, the desert and the mountains." Suddenly across the room he saw a painting that made him gasp. His eyes clouded with tears. "A painting of Noragram! How could you make her so real from an old snapshot? Big Lund, too! I can't believe it! Big Lund looks so real!"

Kips watched guardedly. Would he lose Lundy? Would the boy want to leave Teena and him to return to his eastern home, where his memories of family were so strong? Kips knew this might stir up old wishes, but he felt he owed a debt to this child — to call the past into the present so Lundy could deal better with the future.

Lundy stood before the paintings. He could almost hear the screaming sea gulls and see the ocean, sand dunes, and grasses. Yet suddenly the faces of Great Wind, Nora and Big Lund all blended into one. All three of them were his grandparents.

Impulsively he reached for Teena and lovingly stroked her long black braids. "You have been my mother for all these years and I always will cherish you."

"Little Wind," she answered softly. "You are a part of Big Lund *and* Great Wind. You have the deep blue eyes and the quiet spirit and strength of Big Lund. And as you grow older, you will have the wisdom of Great Wind. My Little Wind," she crooned softly, as she had when Lundy had first come to her.

For a moment everyone was quiet, then Lundy broke the silence. "These faces are powerful reminders of the past. Tonight I see how much I owe Noragram and Lund and Great Wind but also how much I owe to the present — to you and Teena. I know I don't have many friends; it's difficult for me to trust people. But I trusted you, Kips, because you've been the only father I've really known. Someday I will go home, to the ocean, but for now I am your son and your student. I want to learn the wisdom of the past so I can learn to love and live in the future."

Tomanto's usual composure crumpled. "Teena, Teena, what a son we have! Great Wind would have said, 'Little Wind, you make a fine Indian chief.'"

With an abandoned joy, Teena and Tomanto showed Lundy the other paintings — a woman baking bread, a child at play, and Great Wind's horse. There was a painting of a young child — was it Lundy? — building sand castles on the shore. In a corner was a beautiful painting of a young girl with laughing eyes and a determined tilt to her chin. Her breathtaking beauty held Lundy's gaze — until he realized it was Helen.

"That is the only painting I don't like," said Teena, a hint of fury in her voice.

Tomanto motioned for Lundy and Teena to follow him to the other side of the attic where a sheet covered a canvas. When he removed the sheet, Teena cried out in surprise. It was a painting of her as a young woman, in all the color and finery of her native dress. Her dark eyes seemed to gaze into the future. "My Princess," Tomanto said tenderly as he put his arm around Teena's shoulder and pulled her close to him. "Always my Princess."

Lundy was awed by the contrast in the paintings of Teena and Helen. The strokes that created Helen swirled a tempest, but the recreation of Teena left him with a sense of peace. Tomanto watched Lundy's expression — and understood.

"Teena, you are the most beautiful of all," Lundy burst forth. "Someday I hope I meet someone like you." With a rare affectionate display, Lundy caressed Teena's wrinkled face. He knew he would always remember the look of love in Teena's face. The unanswered questions would wait — of why the paintings had not been shown. Someday Tomanto — his beloved Kips — would explain.

Lundy stood at the window with Teena and Tomanto.

"Look, Little Wind, the heavens seem to open up and the moon makes a path through the valley. Just so, a way will be made for you into the future, into your dreams."

With a gallant gesture, Lundy smilingly bowed and gracefully kissed Teena's hand — "Good night, beautiful Princess." While Teena smiled, Lundy turned to Tomanto and said, "Thank you, Kips, for sharing your dream — and your love."

nineteen

Roberto

The crowds cheered as the star comedy bull rider rode into Scottsdale's Parada del-Sol Rodeo. Every year thousands gathered to watch the parade and the cattle drive down Scottsdale Road. Although the animals were really rodeo stock and the cowboys were young businessmen, the visitors loved it.

Helen and Nelson escorted their guest, Roberto Romero, a charming Italian designer and artist through the happy crowd. Roberto had visited New York City, Chicago and Hollywood, but he'd seen nothing in America that could match this vast country of mountains and deserts, sky and sunshine, cacti and flowers. And now this rodeo with the men dressed in their jeans and western bola ties and the women in bright squaw dresses and mocassins impressed him even more.

Helen's delight was boundless but Nelson felt a nagging guilt for leaving Lundy, not only for such long periods of time when they were in Europe, but even today. He should have brought Lundy with them to this celebration. But Helen had insisted that they needed to be free for the sake of Roberto. Nelson made a gallant attempt to shake off his despair when the bands started playing and the governor led the parade in a horse and buggy.

"Twenty-five years ago, this was the one event of the year," Helen explained. "Now we have Arabian horse shows, auctions, classic car auctions, and even concerts."

Roberto was intrigued by the design of the ten-million dollar Renaissance market, a replica of the fourteenth-century Italian town. Helen reminisced about the days when traders came to Scottsdale to shop for ceramics, jewelry, perfumes and handpainted skirts. "In the old days," she said, "deals were settled with a handshake."

Helen continued, "A friend of my grandfather supported the American Indian artists and built pueblo homes for the reservation craftsmen. My grandfather had lavish Navajo rugs and famous paintings in his house. When he died, many of them went to Indian art museums."

Roberto was attentive, caught up with Helen's every word, every gesture. Even as they entered the amateur horse show and joined Edward and Abigail Thornton in the reserved section, Helen was still chatting enthusiastically. "I loved to ride as a child," she laughed, "but I didn't have the patience to discipline myself or my horse. Our servant Kips finally gave up and let me have my way. I'd rather watch a show any day than get dusty and dirty participating."

As they took their seats, Helen studied Roberto's dark, handsome face. His eyes were dashing as they met hers. He had added excitement to their recent European trip — Nelson was always so pensive and reserved, always caught up with the business matters, always anxious to get back home and see how Lundy was doing! As Roberto smiled at her, Helen was glad she had invited him to be their guest. After all, he would add a touch of glamour to the opening of the Thornton Villa, the exclusive retirement village that Nelson and her father had designed.

A band played and the crowd cheered when the master of ceremonies in full dress announced the next contestant. "Little Wind, riding Desert Wind." To the blare of trumpets, Little Wind, dressed as an Indian chief, rode the sleek

Arabian mare as though he had been born in the saddle.

Roberto, thrilled with the pomp and pageantry asked, "Is he a real American Indian?"

"He rides like one," Helen answered. "But sometimes the rider assumes another name for the show." Helen watched intently, admiring the young man's skill. Tomanto — Kips — used to show me those Indian motions when I was a child."

The audience loved Little Wind's performance, and no one was surprised at the final announcement, "The mysterious rider, Little Wind, with his mare, Desert Wind, is the winner." The crowd cheered for a moment, and then, just before the band played, the M.C. startled Nelson and Helen when he said, "This young chief is none other than Lund Lundstrom, son of Nelson Lundstrom of Thornton Enterprises." The spotlight quickly moved to the "reserved" section before returning to Lundy, and then Tomanto in full Indian dress, was introduced as the trainer. Nelson was the first on his feet, clapping and cheering as hard as he could, only wishing the look of pride in Lundy's eye had been his own to share, not Kips's. Nelson smiled and waved at Lundy, who nodded regally, and then at Kips, who bowed his head in appreciation, but not before he'd seen the angry — or was it jealous? — glint in Helen's eye.

Mr. Thornton told Roberto about Great Wind and his friendship with his own father. "Great Wind was one of the great riders of the plains, and many of the beautiful homes and towns of the desert were really monuments to his dream. 'The desert shall bloom,' he often said. "Without his inspiration my father may never have made a go of Thornton Enterprises."

Nelson secretly wished he could have known Helen's grandfather and Great Wind, for their dreams were more in tune with Nelson's plans than with Helen's. She tried to sway her father toward the extreme, modern architecture — and now Roberto was on the scene advocating his bold twenty-first century designs.

Roberto's mind was still on Lundy, and he quickly exclaimed, "I must meet that young man! What poise!" He turned his back to Helen and spoke to Nelson. "How proud you must be of such a son!"

"Thank you. He's extraordinary," Nelson replied, but not before he saw the fury in Helen's eyes.

Although he knew Helen wouldn't like a show of affection in public, Nelson greeted his son with a bear hug. "I am so proud of you Lundy-Boy," he said over and over, and then he clasped Tomanto's hand and, in a broken voice, repeated, "Thank you, Kips, thank you, for all you are to my son." He turned away before anyone could see how deeply he felt. Helen congratulated Lundy and quickly introduced him to Roberto, who praised his performance. "You must enter other competitions," he urged. "You are too good to be an unknown mystery rider."

Roberto's enthusiasm for the entire day filled the evening's emotional gaps. Mr. Thornton suggested they all go out to dinner to celebrate the event, and later they stopped by an outdoor concert at the civic Plaza Mall. This time Lundy was included.

"Tomorrow we go to the Trading Post," Roberto beamed.

It was well past midnight when Helen and Nelson said good-night to their guest and went to their room.

Nelson opened the glass doors to the balcony and looked out across the vast Arizona sky. But in his heart he heard wind in pampas grass and the roll of an ocean on a sandy shore.

Against the background of the star-studded sky, Helen stood in her shimmering blue gown; her hair fell softly around her bare shoulders. Nelson remembered the jealousy in her eyes, and his usual desire to reach for her left him.

He followed her inside, turned away and quietly closed the balcony door. The wind was cold.

twenty

I'll Fly Away

In the summer of 1973 Big Lund and Nora walked hand in hand along the sandy shore. While the ocean rolled in the splendor of a gold sunset, they walked in the security of each other's love. They rested on a favorite old log and watched the ever-changing ocean. For a few minutes they talked of matters of the heart.

"It's hard to believe Lundy is fifteen now. My, didn't he look fine in that picture Tomanto sent — all dressed up in Indian dress, riding Desert Wind?"

Big Lund laughed out loud. "From a Norwegian fisherman to an Indian rider — not bad, eh, Nora-Girl? Not bad!"

"Sometimes I wonder if he'll *ever* want to come home — with all he has in Arizona. My, my, never heard of folks doing so much — riding, skiing, climbing mountains and fishing. But I wonder why he never seems to go to church. It would be easy to forget the past with so much going on every day."

Big Lund smiled sadly. "Strange how we do things we never thought we could do. I never expected to continue in the business alone for this long, but I have been busy. Those college students who've worked for me part-time have surely saved some jobs, and I'm glad I can help them with their bills — and help them find God."

Nora squeezed his hand. "Our Nelson may be away, but now we have many sons who call us Mom and Dad. We have to trust that God will send someone to our Nelson and our Lundy — to guide them to Himself. Strange, isn't it? How God leads just the right people into our lives. Just like the Cranstons. They've brought so much joy to us. That looks like Rebecca running down the beach. Guess it's time we headed home anyhow. My, she is out of breath — running like the wind — crying, too."

"It's Miss Lottie, Nora, Big Lund. It's Miss Lottie," Rebecca struggled for breath. "Miss Lottie was sitting on the porch and my father went over to visit her as he does so often in the evenings. She waved at him and then started her song again, 'I'll fly away — oh glory. I'll fly away.'

"My dad laughed and called, 'Don't fly until I get there.' You know, their joke, but this time when he got to the porch, she was gone. Just sitting there with her head back and her hands folded."

* * *

Sunday afternoon, the church was filled with Miss Lottie's family and friends. She had carefully outlined her funeral and Craig Cranston fulfilled her every wish: "None of that mournful singing, preacher man. This be a glory time. When you hear Miss Lottie did up and fly away, then that be a rejoicing day."

Flowers banked the front of the church as music poured forth in the joyful sound of the old gospel song, "When we all get to heaven." It was as though Miss Lottie dared anyone to weep at her funeral.

"In the sweet bye and bye, we shall meet on the beautiful shore," made the reality of heaven remove the sting of death.

Craig Cranston missed his old friend, but he knew he wasn't really saying good-bye to her. "Miss Lottie's joy infected us all. Her humble beginning, her years of work in the fields or the mill, only drew her soul closer to God. Through her spiritual wisdom she taught us, who were wise in this world, that the greater wisdom is in the fear of God. From her, I learned faith. Because of her my life was changed. Only eternity will tell how many people, especially the young people of our community, have been touched by the joyous life of faith in our Miss Lottie. Almost 98 years of good clean living — most of them walking with the Lord.

"We all smiled when we heard her cane tapping down the walk and her singing, off key, 'I'll fly away.' I used to tease her, 'Miss Lottie you'll do no such thing. You might miss what's going on at Wrightsville Beach.'

"She did fly away, but somehow I have a 'knowing,' Miss Lottie isn't missing a thing. We can't hear her or see her, but from her heavenly rocker she'll be smiling as her young folks sing her song, 'Some glad morning — I'll fly away.' "

* * *

The cars followed Miss Lottie's body to her resting place beside Jake — not far from Melissa's grave. As Mike and Wilma laid flowers on both graves, "Amazing grace," sounded out across the cemetery. Just the way Miss Lottie had requested.

At the Big House, Nora and Wilma fed Miss Lottie's family and friends. "Sharing food and fellowship after a funeral," Miss Lottie always said, "is telling the young folks that life goes on, that sorrow and joy go together. Not too much sorrow, and not too much joy."

It was done just as Miss Lottie would have wanted it.

Late that night Big Lund and Nora watched Craig Cranston walk the beach alone, missing his friend's laughter but humming "Amazing grace," — the song wafting on the wind.

twenty-one

The Journal

It was 1978. The days and months turned into years while the tides ebbed and flowed over the sand of Wrightsville Beach. Nora and Big Lund watched the Cranston children grow up, loving them as their own family. Mike and Wilma Newton came from Richmond for special events while letters coursed between old friends with news of everyday living.

But there were never any letters from Nelson — no answers to the letters sent to him. So often when the phone rang, Nora would glance at Big Lund — hoping, praying. But Nelson never called. Once in awhile now — on rare occasions — there would be a card, postmarked from France or England or some exotic place in the Orient. They always said the same thing: "On business . . . busy . . . Lundy well. Love, Nelson." There was never an invitation to come to Arizona — never a response to their own letters — never the offer to send Lundy home to Wrightsville Beach for the summer.

In their deep pain and loneliness, Nora and Big Lund had turned to the Cranstons. Nora and Carolyn Cranston worked side by side in their gardens and went together whenever they took food and flowers to shut-ins. Over the years a gentle mother and daughter bond grew between them.

Craig Cranston watched over his flock like a tender shepherd. He looked forward to his fishing trips with Big Lund, when they both relaxed and enjoyed their easy relationship. More often than he realized, Craig leaned on Big Lund's common-sense wisdom. His quiet humor and settled faith brought strength and insight to Craig.

On one fishing trip Big Lund seemed pensive. The ocean was calm and the men fished listlessly. "Big Lund, do you remember Miss Lottie saying, 'Holding a fishing pole was a good excuse for doing nothing,'" Craig chuckled. "I still miss her."

Big Lund looked long at the water, then turned to Craig. "I'm thankful to Miss Lottie for sending you to our Nelson's house. You've been like a son to me."

Words seemed superfluous for the moment. Slowly Craig answered, "And you, Big Lund, seem like a father to me, especially since my father Albert died. He was an engineer and never understood or really approved my call to the ministry. You've taught me much about life — and fishing."

Big Lund smiled a slow, easy smile, but came alert when his line pulled taut. He pulled in his fish, then said, "Better pull to shore, looks like the wind's picking up. We'll have fried fish tonight!" With a slap on Craig's back that said more than words, Big Lund headed to shore. It had been a good day.

Late into the night, when most of the lights in the house on the sound were out, Big Lund sat at his desk listening to the wind blow through the pines. The ocean had a restless roll as the waves splashed over the shore.

Big Lund took out his journal and wrote:

> Breathes there a son whose soul is dead,
> Who never to himself has said,
> You are my own — my family,
> You are the ones who loved and cared for me?

You, my son, my only son,
Could you forget the love on one
Who held you gently to her breast
And rocked you into peaceful rest?

What hold is there with awful sway,
Whose power could take your love away,
And turn against your childhood home.
Where have you gone, my only son?

The ocean tide still ebbs and flows.
The seagulls cry; the wind still blows,
And wrestles in the pampas grass.
And life, my son, will too soon pass.

I wing a prayer across the land,
That God in love will stretch His hand
To bring you to the healing place
Of love, forgiveness, and His grace.

In an unsteady hand, he added, "Some say that they will
believe in God when there are answers to life's questions.
I say that I need faith in God when there are no answers.
I believe God that 'Faith is the evidence of things not seen.'
So good night, Nelson, my son. You are loved and forgiven.
Someday we will all understand. Lundy-Boy, you are always
with us. I know time for me is running out but be assured
that I love you."

Big Lund closed the journal, turned out the light, and
slipped quietly into bed beside Nora. He cradled her gently
in his arm as she rested her head on his shoulder. She fell
asleep that way and slept peacefully through the night.

In the morning she awakened early, startled. Instinct, fear
gripped her. She knew before she even turned her eyes to
Big Lund's face that something was wrong. He was very
still, his color pasty. The warmth had drained from Big
Lund. Nora's scream pierced the silence — her cries so long
and loud they woke Craig and Carolyn in the house across
the garden.

* * *

Nora refused to leave the bedside. "Oh, God, let me go with him. Let me go with him," she begged.

Craig Cranston held her gently in his strong arms and wept with her as the mournful cries of the seagulls swept across the dunes, blending with their own.

For Nora Lundstrom, it was the dark night of her soul. The Cranston children followed her like shadows as she walked the lonely beach. She felt Rebecca leaning hard against her, clutching her hand. But Nora was numb — too numb to respond.

It was Mike and Wilma Newton who came first, then Chad on an emergency leave from the Air Force. For hours Chad and Craig Cranston attempted to reach Nelson. His number was still unlisted but they reached the Thornton Enterprises only to be told, "Mr. and Mrs. Lundstrom are away on business — in Europe. No, there's no way for us to reach them."

In frustration, Chad said, "Mr. Lundstrom's father is dead. Now will you put me through to the Thornton Estates?"

There was a moment of hesitation, then the secretary said formally, "Just a moment, Sir."

Chad tapped his fingers impatiently, waiting. He stiffened when he heard the deep, authoritative voice of Edward Thornton saying, "This is Edward Thornton. My secretary just informed me of your loss. May I express my. . ."

"Can we reach Nelson Lundstrom?" Chad interrupted.

"Not until Saturday," he answered curtly. "The Lundstroms never leave forwarding numbers. They were going to rest a few days in Switzerland — Lucerne, I believe — then on to Rome on business. I'll leave a message in our office in Italy for them to call as soon as. . ."

"Never mind," Chad answered. "The funeral will be over by then."

When Nora came in from the beach, she looked questioningly at Chad. "Did you reach my son?" she asked, her voice toneless.

"The Thorntons will try to reach him, Nora. That's all we could do."

She smiled wanly. "I didn't really expect an answer. But thank you for trying, Chad."

* * *

On the day of the funeral, a massive spray of flowers stood at the foot of Big Lund's casket. Chad steadied Nora as she lifted the card and read the name: "Dad, I love you. Nelson."

Chad thought she would faint but she tucked the card back in the envelope and walked away. Chad glanced at Craig Cranston. "I think she knows, Craig," Chad said angrily.

"Knows? Knows what? I thought the flowers were from her son."

"No," Chad whispered as the organ music started. "This is Thursday, remember? They won't even be in touch with Nelson until Saturday."

"Then who — ?"

"Mr. Thornton undoubtedly. A part of his social obligation." Chad's tone was bitter.

"Will you tell Nora?" Craig asked as the little church filled with mourners.

"No, Reverend. That's one truth that I must withhold. Nelson has caused her enough pain."

After the service, Chad and Mike Newton helped carry their friend to his final resting place. Without Nora even asking, Mike stayed on a few weeks to complete Big Lund's unfinished projects — a front porch for one neighbor, new storm windows for another, repair jobs at the grocery store, the finishing touches on the sewing room at the Cranston parsonage. Mike wouldn't take a dime for his labor. "Big Lund would have done the same for me." Then he grinned at Nora, a smile shiny with tears. "I couldn't let that Big Norwegian down. He never left anything unfinished."

During those same weeks, Wilma stayed close to her old friend — sitting quietly, walking the beach with her, talking about the past, reminding Nora that the same heavenly Father who has sustained them when Melissa died would once again comfort Nora.

When the Newtons left, the Cranstons were still there — especially young Rebecca who shadowed Nora everywhere. Rebecca and her mother Carolyn tended the gardens so Nora's flowers would bloom again.

Bert and Craig Cranston spent hours together while Bert, in his young faith, asked questions. He, too, grieved for his old friend and drew closer to his own father. No one knew how deeply Craig missed his friend, Big Lund.

It came to pass, as it always does, that day follows night; the tide ebbs and flows; the rain comes and the sun shines. So the days passed. As Nora sorted through Big Lund's things, she found Big Lund's journal in a desk drawer. On one page she read:

Just finished painting Nelson's house. It is so beautiful. We walked the beach tonight, Nora-Girl, and I was very tired. Remember Nora, I'll always be near you. Nels will come home. Someday Lundy will need you. What a beautiful family! How happy I am to see the lights from Nelson's house. The Cranstons seem like family. Little Bert follows me all over. Little Rebecca will never learn to walk with Miss Lottie and Nora rocking her. What a beautiful baby!

Nora read page after page where Big Lund had poured out his love for her, and his silent grief over Nelson and Lundy. Then the words changed, until the pages seemed to be alive with a new faith and understanding of the sovereignty of God, who works His purposes through the affairs of men. Nora read of the love and forgiveness, the deep faith in God, the power of God's Word and the power of prayer.

At one point Nora read, "We are destined for the throne. Been reading this wonderful book, realizing how precious is the trial of our faith. I'm learning the power of prayer."

At another place, Nora read, "Nelson seems close tonight. Our prayers are getting through. You'll see Lundy-Boy, Nora. Do not give up! I may go before you, my darling, but you must be strong and waiting — waiting for our boys to come home. I love you, my Nora."

And finally, standing out in Big Lund's handwriting, were

the words: "Faith hears the approaching footsteps of God's salvation. Faith rounds out life's day with joy."

Nora clutched the journal to her and quietly wiped her tears with her free hand. Today she would cease her mourning for Big Lund and arise to the challenges ahead.

She went to the dresser and put the journal in the top drawer. Then she peeked out the bedroom window. Rebecca Cranston was cutting across the yard, carrying a spade. When she reached the garden she dropped to her knees by the flower bed.

Nora went down the stairs and outside to the garden and knelt down in the damp dirt beside Rebecca. She caught Rebecca's eyes and smiled. "It's time for me to help you again," Nora said softly. "It's time for me to weed my own flower beds."

Rebecca reached out and touched Nora's face. "Then it's time for singing again, too."

Nora nodded. There was already a melody welling up within her.

twenty-two

The Dream

Lundy's university studies were going well. But he often went home for the weekends. He liked being alone — riding Desert Wind. But he liked being with Tomanto and Teena, too. On Saturdays, Tomanto often had an hour or two free to ride and they'd take off to the hills together.

One Saturday afternoon, Tomanto and Lundy were riding the trail through the valley when Lundy broke the silence. "Why haven't you shown your paintings in public, Kips?"

Tomanto's answer came slowly, guardedly. "It is hard for me to admit, Little Wind, but I fear Miss Helen. I fear her like you do and avoid her like you do."

Lundy tugged at Desert Wind's rein and looked into Tomanto's jet-black eyes. "It is not so much fear, Kips, as — hatred. I do not like my stepmother. I do not trust her." He patted Desert Wind. "My mare is more trustworthy than my stepmother." Lundy laughed — a dry, sardonic laugh. "Helen has kept me from my father. And from my grandparents. I will never forgive her for not allowing me to go back to see Big Lund before he died."

"I know, my son," Tomanto answered, "but you must not hate. It will only destroy you."

"As she is destroying my father?"

"That, too," Tomanto said. "It is her power to destroy that keeps me from showing my art."

"Her power?"

"Yes, Lundy. Miss Helen has power to destroy my art work with her criticism and mocking. And she could fire Teena and me if my art or talent struck her in the wrong way. She does not think it the place of a servant to achieve."

"Nor the right of a stepson."

"She has provided well for you, Lundy."

They rode side by side, their boot toes touching. "But, Kips, you and Teena have provided me with the only thing that counts."

Kips's brow arched quizzically, a lock of thick black hair falling over his broad forehead.

"You provided love, Kips." Lundy urged Desert Wind at a faster pace. "But do not fear Helen's power, Kips. She would never fire you."

"I cannot risk it, Lundy. I need my salary for my people. I teach art to the young people on the reservation. I want them to fulfill their dreams. For them — for now — wisdom dictates that Teena and I guard our secret. I will continue to learn and study — and paint. My day will come, Little Wind, just as your day will come."

They rode on silently for a mile or two, then suddenly Lundy exclaimed, "Kips, I have an idea! We'll have an art showing, under another name — G.W. — Great Wind!" Kips was listening to him intently as Lundy continued. "I have my own bank account and I will be the patron of the anonymous artist. Your day is coming, dear friend! Let me do it. After all, I have learned much from the Thorntons' business ventures."

Tomanto and Lundy's laughter sounded across the valley. It had been a long time since Lundy had been so excited. And he knew exactly where to go for advice and help. One of his university friends, Mark Adams, had invited Lundy home for dinner on several occasions and Mark's mother had talked all evening about her own art show.

Yes, Lundy knew it would work — if only they could keep it all a secret.

* * *

When Helen scanned the morning paper over her second cup of coffee, she called Nelson, in the next room, "We need to call Roberto's townhouse and remind him about the art show today. Look at this advertisement! This artist really must be something. Why won't they say who he is? If I like any, I do want some new paintings for the reception room."

Since Mr. Thornton's heart attack Nelson had been running the company nearly single-handedly. "You go ahead," he answered. "I have appointments all morning and for lunch, but I'll try to meet you at the gallery. Maybe around two?" Still straightening his tie, he gave Helen a hurried kiss as she was dialing Roberto.

"Yes," she said, after Nelson had gone, "let's meet for lunch at twelve at La Rouche."

* * *

Lundy moved casually back and forth through the gallery, eavesdropping on conversations. *If Tomanto could only hear this,* he thought. *And wait until he sees what prices they're going for.*

Lundy was standing in the balcony when he spotted Helen and Roberto walking into the far entrance, He watched them stroll leisurely around the studio, admiring the paintings — lingering in front of them, talking excitedly. Finally they stood just beneath Lundy — so intrigued by the picture in front of them that they failed to notice him. Roberto could not take his eyes off the breathtaking portrait of the young girl with laughing blue eyes and determined tilt to her chin. His comments were unrestrained. "This I buy!" he said. "It is a beauty. What this girl would be as a woman! Like you, Helen, a tempting beauty!" Roberto touched Helen's face seductively. "She reminds me of you, my dear."

Lundy shrank back, shocked.

124

Helen laughed, than gazed back at the portrait. "I had a dress like that when I was a child. But look at that nasty upturned lip — that pout, Roberto. You can have it. I don't like that painting nearly as well as the others. Especially this one," she said, linking her arm in Roberto's and drawing him back to a large-framed painting. "I can't keep my eyes off this Indian Chief and his horse. Such bold colors. Such distinct features. He seems alive. Yes, Roberto, this is the one I want for sure."

As they were standing in the center of the room reviewing what they'd seen, Nelson came in, nearly running, "I'm sorry, I'm late, Helen. Have you two seen everything?"

"Yes, but go ahead. We'll wait," Roberto offered. "You really can't miss this show."

Nelson walked around the room at a steady pace, hardly stopping at any painting until he came to the "Boy and the Sea," the portrait of a child building sand castles on a beach, a golden sunset surrounding him. He stared at it for five minutes, and Lundy heard him ask, "Roberto, what do you think of this one?"

"It's a great piece, Nelson. Go ahead. Buy it."

Helen resisted, her tone restrained. "I don't think it's the artist's best work, Nelson. Why don't we just get the Chief?"

"No," Nelson answered emphatically. "I want this one for my study."

* * *

Later that night, Tomanto grilled his famous steaks on the west patio as Teena quietly served dinner to the Thorntons, the Lundstroms and Roberto. The conversation centered on the art show and the mysterious artist.

"Show me the paintings," Edward Thornton urged. He glanced at Tomanto. "Bring out these works of art that so captivate my family."

Tomanto went into the house and returned with "The Boy by the Sea" and "The Indian Chief." Tomanto placed the pictures along the wall near Thornton. The old man's eyes took in the boy. He winced and turned quickly to the Indian portrait. He gasped when he saw it. "Great Wind?" he whispered.

"Wind?" Helen asked. "Are you in a draft, Daddy?"

"Of course, not," Abigail snapped. "He has his lap robe, his sweater." Her eyes flashed as they met Helen's. She looked back at her husband. "So what do you think of the paintings, Edward?"

"What a shame," he exclaimed, ignoring his wife. He gazed around at the others. "No one knows who this painter is?"

"No, Dad," Helen answered for all of them. "That's what we've been telling you. He just signs himself G.W."

"Here's the other portrait," Tomanto said as he returned with "The Temptress."

When he saw it, Thornton's lips trembled; he gulped for air. "Kips, Kips, please, my medicine." Tomanto disappeared immediately.

Helen pushed back her chair and ran to her father's side. "Are you all right?" she cried. "You look like you saw a ghost, Daddy. What's wrong?"

"No. No. Everything's fine," Edward Thornton protested. "It's just that I've never been so struck by an artist's work." He patted Helen's hand. "You bought 'The Chief' for the reception area?"

"Yes, Daddy. Don't you think it will work well there?"

"Please, Helen, for me — couldn't it go in the library? It belongs there with the books, with the knowledge."

She nodded, reluctantly, puzzled. "I'll have Kips hang it there tomorrow."

"Today, dear. Today." Edward turned toward Roberto. "So 'The Temptress' is yours?" he asked. "Perhaps, you'll sell it to me? Whatever you paid, I'll double it."

Roberto shrugged good-naturedly. His dark eyes flashed. "At *that* price, I cannot resist. The portrait is yours. I'll go back to the art gallery and buy another picture for myself. But," he said, his eyes on Helen, "I shall miss 'The Temptress.' "

Edward Thornton touched the arm of his Indian servant. "Tomanto, will you hang 'The Temptress' in my bedroom? It will humor an old man with a bad heart."

Tomanto nodded, bowed slightly and left the patio — portraits in hand.

* * *

Late into the night, Edward Thornton sat quietly in the library looking into the face of his childhood hero, Great Wind. As he sat near the fireplace, staring up at the portrait, he could see the past more clearly than the present. It was as though he could still hear the Indian Chief, Great Wind, talking to his father. In this same room.

"Some day, the desert will bloom like a rose, dear friend," Great Wind had said. "You and I won't live to see our dreams, but you have your son Edward and I have a grandson, young Tomanto. They will build the dreams we dreamed. They will see our dreams come to pass."

The two men had stood at this same fireplace, facing one another. "My grandson Tomanto draws in the sand and on the rocks, and he carves out figures. Someday he will make my Indian heritage come alive for all the world to see. You, Thornton, your dreams will become buildings made out of the sand and mountains. My dreams will become oil paintings hanging in beautiful homes."

"You have great faith, Great Wind. We Thorntons, we fail that way. . ."

"Faith sees dreams come true," Great Wind said. "Soon I will go to the Land of the Great Spirit, but dear friend, I will always be close to you. We have shared our dreams but our children will fulfill them."

Edward Thornton leaned back in his leather chair. He fought back tears. He thought of the other portrait — the portrait that would hang in his bedroom. *Strange how it all becomes clear tonight,* he thought. *Helen, my daughter — beautiful, spoiled, charming temptress. The very dress I bought for her. So blind — she couldn't even see herself. Poor Nelson — he's sold his soul for my beautiful temptress. Now, as for Lundy, he'll make it, Great Wind. He'll make it with your grandson Tomanto. Oh, Tomanto, dear servant. My father knew you as the young artist but I saw you as only an Indian servant.* Edward shifted his tired body in the chair. *My God, my God, how blind I have been. Forgive me! Great Wind was wiser than I — he sought God.* Suddenly there was a warm sense of peace inside Edward. He wiped the tears from his cheeks. *Tomorrow, I will ask your grandson Tomanto to forgive me. I will set him free to create, to paint. Oh, God, no longer will Great Wind's grandson be a slave, a servant.*

He leaned his head back, his eyes still on the portrait. But the picture of Great Wind blurred and he saw instead, the face of a child. His child. *Oh, my beautiful, Helen, how I loved you. But how wrong I have been — giving in to your every whim — yielding to your devious ways. Forgive me, beautiful temptress, with your flashing eyes and black curls. You did love your father, didn't you?*

He reached out blindly toward Great Wind. *I have peace, Great Wind. For the first time in my life, I have peace.* "God." He spoke the name softly, aloud. "Great Wind, I have found God." He tried to push himself from the chair. "I must find Helen," he said. But he could not move. "Tomorrow then, I will make it right. Tomorrow I will see my Helen. I will talk to Tomanto. But now, I am very tired. . ."

A cloud passed over the moon. The sky darkened.

* * *

When morning came, Tomanto found Edward Thornton still in the library. He reached out to touch him, awaken him, but Tomanto knew at once that Edward Thornton was dead. Thornton's face was turned toward Great Wind's portrait.

Tomanto could almost hear his grandfather say, "Well done, faithful servant. You fulfilled your father's dreams and now your time has come."

He dropped to his knees beside Edward Thornton, weeping. "You were my childhood friend until I became your servant. And then the old friendship was forgotten. Abigail and Helen blinded you. Yet I loved you and served you because of my grandfather, Great Wind." Tomanto stood up. He folded Edward Thornton's cold hands in his lap. He smiled down at the still form. "You knew, didn't you? Last night you recognized the artist. You saw me for who I really am."

Tomanto turned from the chair and went quietly out of the room. He must find Miss Abigail, and Miss Helen, and tell them. Tell them what? he wondered. That Edward Thornton was dead? No, he would tell them that Edward Thornton was at peace.

twenty-three

Turning Homeward

In the next few days, Nelson quickly wearied of all the details and concern for formality. He wondered if anyone really grieved over the death of Edward Thornton.

Abigail Thornton carefully planned each detail of the funeral. Teena and Tomanto carried out her wishes, while Helen wept like a child. How could this happen? Her father had always recovered before. He had been there to grant every wish. Now he was gone.

Only at the reading of the will did Helen's tears cease. They were replaced with a fury that caught Nelson off guard.

Expressing his trust in Nelson's business expertise, Edward Thornton had turned over the control of the Thornton Enterprises to Nelson. Helen had lost out to the one she wanted to control. She smoldered. She remembered her father having a conference with his lawyers shortly after his first heart attack. So this is what he had been up to? How dare he!

But what was worse, Lundy was to be beneficiary to a large amount. Teena and Tomanto received the cottage for their lifetime as a reward for their faithfulness. It was true that both she and mother Abigail were amply provided for — they would never lack financially. The lavish Thornton estate was in Abigail's name; the Lundstrom home in Helen's. But there was no joy for Helen. No real gratitude — people she had thought beneath her had shared in the inheritance.

Nelson never thought the business responsibilities could increase so rapidly. He was engrossed in the work, eager to succeed. He wanted to prove to Helen that Edward Thornton had chosen well. As Nelson's work burden became increasingly heavy, a lonely weariness engulfed him. His thoughts repeatedly turned homeward. But since his father's death, he had been ashamed to journey back to Wrightsville Beach. He had neglected his family, his roots. Faith and family ties had slipped through his fingers over the years.

He would not allow the Thornton Enterprises to be lost. He would make Helen proud of him and cause Abigail to acknowledge his skills. Time moved swiftly around him, while the hours lay heavy on his soul. Before he realized it, two years had passed. Lundy was graduating from the university!

Nelson longed to have Lundy join him as a business partner but he feared that Lundy belonged to another world — a world created by Tomanto. He couldn't hope for his son to enter his world when he had turned away from Lundy in his time of need. June, 1981 — how fast the years had gone! How much opportunity he had lost.

Helen was slipping away from him, too. He realized now that since her father's death, Helen was finding her emotional comfort in Roberto's warm, impulsive nature. She spent day after day with Roberto scheming and dreaming with him on the interior design for the extension on the Thornton Villa — Abigail's expensive tribute to Edward Thornton's memory.

Nelson had cornered Helen a week before Lundy's commencement exercise. "You will be there, Helen, won't you? Lundy's expecting us both."

Helen gave a toss of her head, her eyes defiant. "Lundy doesn't care who attends his graduation as long as Teena and Kips are there."

Nelson winced. "But you will be there?"

"If I'm back from the buying trip in time."

"Buying trip?"

"Yes, Roberto and I are picking up some art pieces for the villa."

Nels knew then that she would miss graduation. He wasn't surprised when she called at the last minute. "Darling," she said breathlessly, "Roberto and I have been delayed. But we'll be home in time for the party this evening. We wouldn't miss Mother's celebration for Lundy."

No, Nelson thought bitterly. *You wouldn't miss Abigail's social. You always shine at those. It'll be another chance to make a fool of me — to dance in the arms of Roberto — to flaunt your defiance, your contempt for Lundy and me.*

At commencement, Nelson sat with Teena and Tomanto. Just before the ceremony began, Abigail slipped in and sat beside Nelson. She leaned over and whispered, "Everything's ready for tonight's party. I've included several of the more attractive debutantes. Lundy should be pleased."

Nelson nodded absently, thinking, *It's a wonder Lundy even agreed to attend. Surely he realizes you intend to promote a good marriage — that you think him valuable to the Thornton Enterprises.*

"It's the social event of the year, Dad," Lundy had teased. "Me so handsome and all. I guess I just fit right into Abigail's plans. At least I made it on her social calendar."

"But don't you want to be with your friends?" Nelson had asked.

"Not this time. I'd rather be with you, Dad." Lundy's expression had still been serious when he added, "Besides, Dad, Edward Thornton has been dead for two years now. Abigail has been looking for the proper excuse to have one of her famous parties." He gripped Nelson's shoulder. "Let's not disappoint her."

The music was building to a rising crescendo; the graduating class was marching in.

* * *

Teena and Tomanto sat up proudly. Tomanto nudged Nelson as Lundy paraded by them.

Teena dabbed her tears, remembering so many years ago when the young child had come to the Thornton home. Little Wind was now a man.

Had he really been a frightened child? she wondered. Had he really refused to cry in front of Miss Helen? Did he still remember the Indian lullaby she crooned to him? She was so proud of him. Of his horsemanship at thirteen. Of his unselfish act of love in planning the art show for her Tomanto. His kindness to Abigail at Mr. Thornton's death.

She stole a glance at Lundy's father. Nelson could not take his eyes from his son. She ached for Mr. Lundstrom. When he took over the Thornton Enterprises, Teena had whispered to him, "Say a prayer for yourself, Mr. Lundstrom. You will have many long, hard days ahead."

He had looked at her, his handsome face twisted. "I've forgotten how to pray, Teena," he had answered sadly.

Now Teena's gaze settled on Abigail Thornton's stoic face. Her eyes met Teena's. She nodded curtly and turned away but not before Teena caught the pain and loneliness in her expression. Did she regret it now — not having that son that Edward Thornton always wanted? Was she swallowing her words, "One child is enough?" Until this moment, Teena hadn't thought much about it. But it had been Abigail's decision not to bear another child. And now as she watched Lundy Lundstrom move jauntily across the stage for his diploma, did Abigail realize that it could have been her own grandson, a Thornton? Abigail Thornton barely knew Lundy. But Teena was certain she had plans for him.

After the ceremony, Lundy made his way toward them. He smiled at Abigail and reached out impulsively to hug Nelson. For one brief moment, father and son were one. Then Lundy turned to Tomanto and handed him the diploma. "We did it, Kips," he said proudly. *"WE* did it."

Teena knew there were changes coming. Lundy would never go for the Thornton Enterprises — for Abigail's control. Eventually he would make his way home to the North Carolina coast. Then her beloved Tomanto would be free — his work at the Thornton Estates would be complete. He could give full time to his painting and art shows. At last Teena would be free to go home to the reservation. She wanted to go home where she was comfortable in her long braids and moccasins. Tomanto could show his art proudly and she would indeed be a princess to her people.

* * *

As they promised, Helen and Roberto arrived in time for the festive dinner, prepared by Tomanto and Teena. They seemed genuinely sorry that they'd been late and presented Lundy with a large gift that was the shape of a picture frame.

"I know it's hard to conceal what it is," said Roberto. "But open it. I think you'll still be surprised."

Lundy was pleased. When he looked up, he saw that Teena's eyes were dancing with delight. Although no one had admitted that Tomanto was the anonymous artist, Teena was no longer afraid to show her pride. Only Tomanto remained impassive. He remembered painting the sunset — portraying the close of a day, and the close of a season. He had felt a sadness at the passing.

* * *

Hours later when the party was over, Lundy walked into the library with Nelson. As soon as Lundy walked into the room he gasped. Tomanto's "Boy and the Sea" was hanging where "The Chief" had been.

After a long silence, Nelson said, "We'll put 'The Chief' back up. I just wanted you to see this picture in the best setting of the house. It reminded me of you and Wrightsville Beach, and I couldn't resist. I wanted you to have it. I just wish I knew who the anonymous artist was."

Lundy studied the painting again. "Look again, Dad. Don't you recognize the boy?"

Nelson stared at Lundy and then the painting. "It really is you! But how? What's the story?"

"Tomanto, Dad. He did them all. I'm sure Mr. Thornton recognized 'The Chief' — and 'The Temptress' — the night he died. You remember 'The Temptress'?" He paused. "Do you see Helen in that one?"

"Helen? My wife?"

"It's a long story, but Tomanto has had to hide his talents. He was afraid of Helen."

Nels grew old in moments, and in his sadness, he drew Lundy to him. "Forgive me, Lundy. Forgive us both."

Slowly the two men walked toward the kitchen door and out into the night. The emotional moments had melted the distance of the years, and father and son walked together with a deep understanding of life. The years could not be erased, but the two men could face the present with thanksgiving.

They circled the drive and walked to the south end of the property, and then as they walked back toward the house, Lundy was the first to see two forms locked in an embrace — an embrace so passionate that he wanted to look away. Lundy wished the moon would go dark so no one — especially his father — would see the lovers. But before Lundy could pull his father in another direction, Nelson saw Helen and Roberto.

Nels stopped abruptly. "I've been a fool," he cried out. "I trusted her. And she has betrayed me."

In the still night air, Helen heard Nelson groan. She turned from Roberto's arms in time to see Nelson go limp against Lundy.

* * *

Nelson was placed in a special care unit, with nurses around the clock. Only his eyes were pleading. He couldn't speak, couldn't feel.

Whenever Helen appeared, Nelson grew restless, agitated. The doctor advised her to return home. "The nurses will take good care of Mr. Lundstrom," he assured her.

But Lundy stayed at his father's bedside.

The days and weeks flowed together. After long sessions of therapy, Nelson's speech improved, but the paralysis on his right side continued.

"In my trunk in the attic is a Bible, your mother's Bible," Nelson said one day. "Don't let Helen see it, but bring it to me. Read it to me, please."

Repeatedly, Lundy read the twenty-third Psalm and John

14. He read passages that Melissa had underlined. He read the poems that were on the bookmarks and quotes that were written on the blank pages in the front. Nelson healed slowly. Gradually a quiet peace replaced the pain.

"Lundy, I asked God to forgive me, but I must be sure you have forgiven me. I've been such a fool, selling my soul for passion and power. Both are fleeting, and only true love remains. God's love is real, Lundy. I knew that once — long ago. I also knew the love of a beautiful woman, your mother Melissa. How she loved us both! When she died, I died! I closed out the love of others, my parents, the Newtons, you. My eyes were blind, and my heart was stone.

"Melissa and my Lundy both . . . forgive me, forgive me."

Lundy took his father's hand. He seemed so frail — suddenly old. "I love you, Dad. Of course, I have forgiven you."

"Read the Lord's prayer, Lundy, that part about forgiving us our trespasses, as we forgive those who trespass against us.

Lundy didn't know the prayer by heart, but he thumbed through the gospels until he found the section, which Melissa had underlined.

After he'd read it once, Nelson asked him to read it again. Finally, he said, "Lundy, tell Helen I want to see her. She must know that I forgive her. Please, Lundy, forgive her also — for only then can God forgive us."

Nelson grew quiet, as though asleep. Lundy waited, but thought, *I'll never forgive her, Dad — not for what she's done to us.*

As though reading his thoughts, Nelson's eyes opened. "Forgive Lundy-Boy. It's the only way to be forgiven. For the first time since your mother's death I have peace, real peace. Tell Mother how much I love her. Ask her to forgive me." The conversation had visibly tired Nelson and he paused a long time again before going on. "The lawyers came today. I turned the business over to Helen and the lawyers. I made ample provision for my mother. Pray God she'll forgive me. I am a wealthy man, Lundy-Boy, but I was richer than a king when I was home with you and Melissa on the sound."

The silence was even longer this time.

" 'Now I lay me down to sleep' — I used to say that to

you when you were a baby. 'I pray the Lord my soul to keep.' Lundy-Boy, go home. Go home to your Noragram." Nels stirred restlessly. "One more thing, son . . . promise me . . . bury me beside Melissa. Beside my Big Lund. Take me home, son. Take me home."

twenty-four

The Journey

The plane rose into the billowing clouds, veiling the Arizona desert. Lundy sat beside Tomanto, his eyes closed. For the first time in seventeen years, he was on his way back to Wrightsville Beach. But there was no joy. They were taking Nelson Lundstrom's body home for burial.

Strange how he suddenly remembered the kind lady on his first plane trip. "You'll see your grandmother again," she had said. "The years will go fast."

He already knew that Craig Cranston had read his telegram to Noragram and together they had made the arrangements to meet the plane, to have a memorial service at the Community Church.

Lundy was confident that word was spreading throughout the sound: "Nelson Lundstrom is coming home; Nora will see her Lundy-Boy again."

Lundy's thoughts skimmed over the last week. His dad had slipped into a coma; three days later he was gone. Knowing that his father hadn't spoken again to Helen, Lundy gave her his message. "My father forgave you," he had told her bluntly.

"Forgave me?" she said with disdain. "For what? Where would your father have been without me?"

Lundy had bit his lip, then exploded. "Helen, you've always taken anything and everything you wanted, but now I am taking my father home where he belongs. I'll bury him beside my mother who really loved him."

"I forbid it," she countered.

"Don't." His heart had pounded as it was doing now. "How my father could forgive you is beyond me. But I can't. I won't. Now get out of this room, Helen, and I'll make arrangements for my father."

Something in the tone of his voice convinced her. "Go then. There's really no place for him in the Thornton family plot anyway." She was crying, angry. "Take your beloved father and bury him at the beach."

"I will," Lundy had answered.

In her hysteria, she had managed a defiant smile. "And I'm going to Italy — to Roberto — where I can forget this place and have some fun again. Love," she laughed bitterly, "what is it? Take your father to Melissa. That's where his heart has always been. He was never really truly mine."

Tomanto and Lundy were still flying high above the clouds. In less than an hour they would be at the New Hanover Airport in Wilmington, North Carolina. "Tomanto," Lundy broke the silence. "Were you afraid to love?"

"To love Teena?" He seemed surprised. "Never."

"But it takes so much trust. I don't think I'll ever marry."

"Unless you find someone like my Teena."

Lundy laughed dryly, running his hand through his thick blond hair. "Do you think I would do well with an Indian maiden?"

"Yes, if she loved you."

Kips turned his sun-wrinkled face to Lundy. "Do not judge your father too harshly. He was a gifted administrator — a man of politics and business. He made the Thornton Enterprises into an empire. But in the affairs of the heart, he was sadly lacking, my son. Lundy, someday you may be tested in the same areas of strength or weakness. Learn from the past, Little Wind."

"I loved my father..with all his rejection of me, I loved him. But Helen..."

"Lundy, you mustn't judge women by what you've seen in Helen. If it hadn't been for my Teena, I would have quit painting when Great Wind died. Teena gave me back my love for life . . . and my gift." He touched Lundy's arm. "When a man can't feel, he dies. That's what happened to your father when he lost your mother. His emotions turned to steel. Helen Thornton was able to stir his emotions again. Her passion rekindled his manhood. For that, try to remember her with less bitterness."

"Helen destroyed my father."

"Be careful, Little Wind. Temptation comes at unexpected moments. There are many women like Helen. Desire controls them. There was a time when Mr. Thornton was not controlled by Helen or by his wife Abigail. He loved a beautiful, gentle girl who worked in his father's household. Edward was at the university and this college girl came as a companion and secretary to his mother. They fell in love and planned to marry. But because of social pressure, Edward Thornton abandoned her and married the socialite debutante of the year, Abigail. He became a slave to her."

"And the girl that he loved?" Lundy asked.

"She bore Edward's son out of wedlock. Later she married an understanding man who gave the child his name. Mr. Thornton never knew about the child."

Lundy sat in silence, staring at the sun-filled clouds. Finally he asked, "What if I choose the wrong woman, Kips?"

"Learn from your father's mistakes, Lundy. Find a woman like your own mother, gentle and selfless in her love for you. Someone who will comfort you in your failure and urge you to reach for your dreams. And when you've found her, love her. Love her always."

"Someone like your Teena."

"Yes, even if she, like my Teena, is not able to live in the glory of your success. My dear one has lived only for my achievement. Her only desire has been to see my art acclaimed, and now that it is, Teena wills to die, to be with her people. She has been so good to me, Lundy. Now I must not push her to travel the country with me. Teena cannot enter the world of success, so I have determined to enter her world and live on the reservation and teach the young. I must die to my soul's hunger for world travel, but I will be content — for the sake of Teena."

"You are stronger than I am, Kips."

"There is peace and strength in true love, and you will find it, Little Wind. You are wealthy now, but you will be truly wealthy when you have found a true love."

The seat belt sign flashed on. Kips reached for the strap to comply. "There are different kinds of love, as there are different kinds of women. Remember that, my son. But remember too that the love between friends knows no barriers. You may be miles from me, Little Wind, but you will never be far from my heart. You helped my art dream come alive. You helped make me a wealthy man so I can help educate the children of my own people. We owe each other a great debt."

"My debt is the greater, Kips."

"No matter, my son. I know you will search for the wisdom of the Great Spirit, just as I have, and if you find truth, you must come to me and share it, for my heart yearns for truth."

* * *

As the jet rolled to a stop at New Hanover Airport, Lundy spotted his beloved grandmother. Noragram, surrounded by her beloved pastor's family and her friends from the sound, watched silently as the body of her son was carried from the plane. Lundy ached for her. She was weeping now, as a gentle August breeze tugged at her gray hair.

Then Noragram's eyes turned toward Lundy. Did she think him tall, blond, handsome like Big Lund, like his dad, Nelson? Lundy wondered. Would she be glad to see him?

Just as he reached her, she stretched out her arms to greet him. He bent low, crushed her to him and wept.

For Nora, there were no words, only a sad joy, an over-whelming awareness of God's peace engulfing her. Her son — and her grandson — were home. Miss Lottie had been right, "Don't you fret, Nora. Someday, in God's good timing, Nelson and Lundy-Boy will be coming home."

twenty-five

The Sunrise of Truth

Tomanto sat quietly beside Lundy and Nora on the front row of the church. Holding Nora's hand, on the other side, was Rebecca Cranston. Rebecca's mother, Carolyn, her grandmother, Sara, and young Bert filled out the pew. Wilma, Mike and Chad sat across the aisle.

The organist played the old hymns of the church while the people streamed in to pay their respects. Nora's wish had been granted: Nelson's service at the church, just as Big Lund's and Melissa's had been.

This was their church — the place where Nelson and Melissa had been married, where Lundy-Boy had been dedicated. Nora found peace in the familiar surroundings.

The years had soothed the sting of death, but the longing for Big Lund never left Nora. For years she had clung to her faith in God that Nelson would come home. Now her only son was at peace, at home with the Lord, with Melissa, and with Big Lund. He was loved and forgiven.

As for Lundy-Boy, my how he looked like Big Lund! Lundy held Nora's hand in his and seemed to be a child again, secure in his Noragram's love. The present and past floated like clouds in the sky. He vaguely remembered the old hymns and the inside of the church. Big Lund had slipped peppermints to him here during the long sermons. Although he missed Big Lund his presence was everywhere, even here at church. The old hymn, "Savior Like a Shepherd Lead Us," brought back the story about the Good Shepherd, which he'd never quite forgotten. Some how he felt like the lost sheep. It was strange how much he could remember, since he hadn't been to church in years. Reading Melissa's Bible to his father had brought some of the images back and suddenly he remembered his father's words: "Forgive Helen, as the Father in heaven forgives us."

Tomanto sensed the tension in Lundy and quietly gave his hand a reassuring grip. The Indian's piercing black eyes took in the old frame church and worn pews, but his heart took in the warmth and worship of the people. He had never been in a church like this before — only in the rigid stone and stained glass church the Thornton's attended for weddings and concerts.

These people worship a Great Spirit in a humble building, he thought. *The Thorntons paid tribute to man's glory etched in stone. Strange, how lonely I feel. I have wealth, and recognition as an artist, my faithful Teena — yet, I am lonely.*

Tomanto listened attentively to the tenor soloist:

> I saw your hand outstretched for me;
> I saw your love from Calvary;
> I looked — and then I turned away.
> I wanted, oh, so much to live;
> I thought the world had much to give.
> I looked again, but then I walked away.
>
> I never knew that I could cry so many tears;
> I never knew that I'd be counting wasted years.
> I need redeeming grace,
> That Calvary love that took my place.
> I'm turning 'round to see
> That outstretched hand for me.

I never knew that I could feel so all alone;
I never knew that I would reap what I had
sown;
I'm coming back to You.
My lonely days and nights are through;
I'm turning 'round to see
Those outstretched hands for me

I'm coming home; I'm coming home; I'm
coming home.
I'm so tired of trying to make it on my own;
I'm coming home to You.
My lonely days and nights are through;
I'm turning 'round to see
Those outstretched arms for me.

Touched by the power of the words, Lundy gripped Tomanto's arm. He was torn between hate for Helen and love
for his father — now love for his father's God who was
calling him home to the heart of God. No. He wasn't ready.
He couldn't let go of the hate he felt toward Helen for
killing his father. The moment passed. His heart grew cold.

Tomanto tried to swallow the lump in his throat. *So this
was the hunger in my heart?* he wondered, *the longing for
the Great Spirit? To know this love must be to have more
wealth than anyone, for this is a love even better than a
woman's.*

Craig Cranston interrupted Tomanto's thoughts. "We don't
know who wrote that song, but it was discovered in Big
Lund's journal, and requested today by Miss Nora."

Craig continued. "We are not here today to bury the dead,
but to honor the memory of Nelson Lundstrom, who is not
dead, but alive forevermore. We all understand the dangers
of our ocean's riptides, but we often fail to understand the
dangers of life's riptides. For a short time Lund was caught
in life's riptide but he came home, home to God and home
to Wrightsville Beach where he will be remembered as the
son who returned to the faith of his father and mother. No
man is at home until he is at one with God."

Craig's eyes lingered on Lundy and his Indian friend Tomanto. "Men search for truth all over the world, only to discover that the Sunday school song says it all, 'Jesus loves me this I know.' No one comes to God the Father, except through the redemptive love and grace of Jesus Christ, who is the only way. Nelson came this way."

Tomanto's heart burned within him. *Is this man Jesus the God who became one of us and died?* his heart cried out.

Tomanto knew the story from the art he'd studied, the literature he'd read, but only now did the light of eternal truth begin to rise in his heart.

Craig continued, " 'I am the resurrection and life, he that believeth in Me shall never die.' Believing is more than acknowledging the historical fact of the death and resurrection of Jesus Christ; it involves receiving into your heart the redemptive grace of God. For a time Nelson Lundstrom faltered in his faith, but in the end he sought his Redeemer, and he found his peace.

"Nelson Lundstrom saw the glory of God in the heavens and in the firmament, God's handiwork. We don't need faith to see, but we need faith to acknowledge our sin and receive the grace of God. We thank God today that to every man is given a measure of faith — enough to believe. . ."

Craig looked down from the pulpit, his eyes shining. "Nora Lundstrom prayed for her son — agonized for him. She believed that God would keep His word and bring her son home. Her prayer was not answered in the way that she expected. But she rejoices today that her son is home — face to face with his Redeemer."

Like a soft breeze from the ocean came the breath of faith into Tomanto's spirit. "I believe, Great Spirit of God. Your Son died for me, Tomanto. He is Truth! Now He is my Way."

Light, like the sun at high noon, exploded into Tomanto's heart.

* * *

One by one the cars left the cemetery to meet at the Big House where neighbors and friends remembered the past together. Long tables covered with food sent in by friends expressed their love for Nora, a reminder that living continues.

Later, Tomanto left the crowd at the Big House, to walk alone by the rolling ocean. Until this week he had never heard the ocean or watched the dying rays of the setting sun reflected from the white-capped waves. He had never heard the wind blow through the dune grasses. He drank in the mystery of these sounds and sights, walking until he stood at the inlet, alone with the sky and sea. He stood still for several minutes, not knowing exactly how to speak to the Great Spirit who had found him and called him. Then, he stretched his arms to heaven and spoke into the wind, "I, too, have come home — home to You, the Great Spirit of earth, sky and sea. There is much to understand and learn about your Son, Jesus, but in my heart I know Truth. Soon I must go home to Teena. My people must know this Truth."

He walked into the sunset with the golden glow on his bronzed skin. In the distance he saw young Rebecca Cranston coming toward him. "A beautiful strange child," he mused, "so beautiful, like spring and violets." For a moment Tomanto ached for his youth.

Rebecca ran toward him, golden hair ablaze with the glow of the sunset. Her bare feet flew over the sandy shore, while the sea gulls screamed from the sky. With the abandonment of a happy child she threw her arms around him and Tomanto noticed tears on her cheeks. "Tomanto, I know, I know. I saw your face. I saw Jesus in your face. You saw Him. I know you saw Him as the Truth. Oh, Tomanto, I prayed for you." Softly she added, "and I prayed for Lundy, but he turned away."

"You prayed for us?" Tomanto stroked her golden hair and wondered how it would have been to have such a daughter. Gently he brushed her tears. "You prayed for me? Why?"

Slowly she raised her eyes, blue as robin's eggs. "Tomanto, it is because you love him, Lundy-Boy, and I love you for loving him. Do you understand?"

As Tomanto walked beside her, her hand rested on his arm. "Ah, you are but a child, my golden princess, a young fawn, soft and beautiful. What do you know about God and prayer?"

"We all come to God as children," she answered softly. "Some are older children, like you, but I came to God as a young child. He is very real to me. Besides I am sixteen years old, almost seventeen, and that's not a child." Her laughter sounded like the notes of a happy symphony.

"My little princess, you are right. You are not a child — you have the wisdom of the ages in you. Today I heard Truth, and I, too, believe God. I became a child. I walked alone with Him and I am at peace. But, my little one, why Lundy-Boy?"

Tomanto's black eyes looked deeply into the soul of Rebecca Cranston. Without flinching, her blue eyes met his gaze and her unspoken answer looked deeply into the soul of Tomanto, the artist. For a moment they stood in silence, too deep for words. Then, "I love Lundy-Boy, Tomanto. I love him, and I always will."

An arrow pierced Tomanto's heart, for he knew this strange child held a love in her heart like Teena and Melissa. But he knew that Lundy could not love until he relinquished hate. Tenderly Tomanto crooned an old Indian love song. "Great Spirit of earth, seas and sky, watch over this little fawn for arrows must not wound my golden princess. Open the eyes of my son, Lundy-Boy, to know Truth." With a quiet peace, they walked hand in hand, father and daughter in spirit.

"Tomanto, I have always loved him. I live in his house, and I have his room where the cradle stands. I even talked to him when I played make believe, as a little girl. I pray for him every night. When I saw you and Lundy get off the plane, I knew then that I loved him, and it was no make believe. Today I saw the light of God in your face and I knew that you believed. I also saw the shadow come over Lundy, but someday, Tomanto, someday, he too, will believe.

Such wisdom, he thought. *So much like my Teena.*

"Tomanto, I love you for loving him and thank you for taking care of him."

"I must return to Teena and my people soon," he said,

"But before I go I must do a painting of you by the sea. We will call it, 'My Golden Princess.' Someday you can give it to Lundy-Boy."

They walked in silence while the sun slipped behind the horizon and the ocean rolled in ceaseless rhythm.

twenty-six

The Painting

T he sun marched with the majestic splendor of a king, enthroned in the heavens, dispatching stars behind the skies of the morning. Every crevice of earth was touched by the imperial monarch. Desert sands burned under the ruling king, while mountain flowers reached up from hidden valleys for warmth and light.

Tomanto stood on the shore, his arms outstretched to the sky, his spirit, soul and body in total worship — not of the sun, but of the God who created the sun.

Once he had worshiped the sun, moon and stars, but felt only a loneliness within, even though his mind was in awe of the power of earth, sea and sky. Today he was at peace with God, the great I Am!

He set up his easel and as he looked out over the ocean, he contemplated the past days and wondered about the tomorrows. He had left Lundy in the gardens with his beloved grandmother. Together they were walking the familiar lanes into the past, where Big Lund's presence seemed real again. Tomanto understood.

He watched them go to the house where Lundy had hidden from Helen and Nelson before they snatched him from his grandparents. Rebecca's house now. Tomanto smiled to himself. A cloud hid the sun for a moment, and Tomanto wondered how long it would be before Lundy really came home.

Last night Nora had shared Big Lund's journal with Tomanto and the words of wisdom had leaped from the pages. "Don't weep, wise grandmother," Tomanto had urged gently, "but protect this journal for Lundy to read when he is ready. It is necessary for him to return to the West, to bring order to his affairs before coming home. I will be with him. Our Lundy must journey into the past to live in the present and prepare for the future."

Tomanto remembered how frail Nora looked, but he knew the Great Spirit would protect her. Looking out over the sun-kissed waves, Tomanto was moved by the memory of Nora's heartfelt thanks to him for his care over Lundy. She was grateful for every letter, picture and word of encouragement when loneliness had overwhelmed her and Big Lund.

He could almost see her tear-stained face and feel her hand on his forearm as she'd said, "Tomanto, you are truly my own son. How I love you and Teena! Tell her how much I love her. Take this quilt I made and let her remember that God's love covers her like a blanket. I will always love and pray for you and Teena. Please return, Tomanto. I must see your face again before I go home. I can't go home before Lundy-Boy comes home — really home."

She had gazed out over the beach and ocean before adding, "I always know when a storm is coming for first comes the wind. A storm is coming Lundy's way. God help him. Bring him home!"

Quietly Tomanto echoed the words of last night, "Bring him home, Great Spirit, even if the wind comes first to blow the chaff away."

He set up the brushes and paints and turned to his canvas. With strokes of love, he outlined the frail form of Nora, with her faithful dog Browser beside her. Face to the wind, she walked with her head held high. She walked in sunlight, with the shadows behind her. He named the painting, "Face to the Wind." Finally he stood back. "God will bring Lundy home, wise grandmother, he spoke out loud. "I, too, will return again."

In the evening Tomanto returned to the beach, this time with Rebecca. Against the golden rays of the sunset, she sat on a boulder with her sun-tanned arms wrapped around her knees. From under a full skirt, her sun-tanned feet peeked out, resting on a rough ledge. Blowing in the breeze her golden hair reflected the sun's splendor. But it was her blue eyes that Tomanto caught with the strokes of his brush. Looking far out to sea he saw the love and longing of a beautiful girl for her lover. Her tilted chin spoke of her faith — to wait.

A step behind him made Tomanto turn to see Lundy looking over his shoulder. "She looks like she's waiting for someone, Kips," Lundy commented.

Kips put his brush down and answered softly, "She is."

Blind to its meaning, Lundy called Rebecca, "Let's go for a run on the beach, Little One."

Tomanto watched them run in the sunset and called out to the wind, "Great Spirit, open Lundy's eyes."

In his heart he knew that the "Golden Princess" would be his finest work of art. In this picture was the sea, earth and sky, and the glory of youthful innocence and trusting love. In the painting of Nora, "Face to the Wind," was ageless wisdom and faith. Someday he would show the paintings to the world.

Slowly he packed his brushes and, with the easel under his arm, he faced the rolling ocean. Lundy and Rebecca were racing the waves. Like the tide, Lundy's life had ebbed and flowed — sometimes rushing toward the shoreline, toward home, at other moments it rolled back to the ocean's depths, to life's uncertainties.

Tomanto felt the cool of the early evening breeze. He watched it blow the clouds across the sinking sun. *When,* he wondered, *will the clouds be blown from Lundy's life?*

Tomanto turned back to the Big House. Tomorrow he would prepare to return to Arizona, to Teena and the valley. It was where he belonged.

twenty-seven

The Valley

Tomanto and Lundy were silent as their jet lifted high above Wilmington, North Carolina, and winged its way into a never-never land of sun-filled clouds. Lundy finally broke the silence. "Part of me belongs there, Kips, yet another part of me is in Arizona. I feel lost — empty here. My mother and father, even Big Lund, are gone. Even my childhood friend, Miss Lottie, is dead. My house is filled with other people — still I felt at peace when Rebecca showed me each room and told me how she slept in my cradle as a baby. Strange how peaceful that house seemed to me — like home! The Thornton mansion could hold four houses in one, yet it was never home. I felt more at peace in the cottage with Teena and you."

"Ah, it was Teena's cooking!" Tomanto laughed.

Lundy closed his eyes for a minute then opened them. "Did I tell you, Kips, I was shocked when I found out Rebecca's grandmother was the Aunt Sarah I met on the plane seventeen years ago? Her grandmother thought Helen was beautiful." Lundy added bitterly, "But not inside, Kips — inside she wasn't beautiful. I still hate Helen, Kips. When I saw her in Roberto's arms I resolved to get revenge. I can't get away from that."

Tomanto remained silent, quietly asking for the wisdom of the Great Spirit. Slowly he answered, "My son, the child of my heart, listen to my words of wisdom. Hate only destroys you, but renders no harm to Helen. Revenge turns inward to bitterness. People like Helen pay dearly in later life. They need mercy, not hate. Mercy and forgiveness will return to bless you in many ways, but hate will return to destroy you, my son.

"You must ponder well, my Lundy-Boy, for I will not speak often on this matter. You, alone, must make the decision. Emotions are an untrustworthy pendulum, swinging back and forth. To forgive as we are forgiven brings us to the act of the will. Will to forgive, Lundy."

Lundy heard with his ears, but his heart remained cold, producing more darkness in his soul. He felt powerless to open the door to light.

Kips saw the tortured face and suffered for him. He vowed to love this son with unconditional love and understanding. Placing his big brown hand over Lundy's clenched fist he added gently, "This is a battle you must win, and you will win! Love is stronger than hate and I know you have a great capacity to love. Just don't close your heart to Teena and me for we love you more than life itself."

Deeply moved by Tomanto's words, Lundy grabbed his hand — "Oh, Tomanto, I'll always love you and Teena and I'll never go away from you or your wisdom. Help me, Tomanto, help me! I feel so numb."

Tomanto seemed to hear Great Wind's words coming from the past: "Avoid the depth of dark water, my son; step only in the light, for pebbles will glisten in the sunlight. So come thoughts to give light over a stony path. Tread gently with the dark night of man's soul. Step only in the light until a way is clear."

Tomanto seemed to be a child again sitting beside the Great Chief by the open fire. "Oh my grandfather, what are the pebbles of light for this troubled youth?"

"A man and his horse learn much from each other. The valley and the mountains speak of greater healing than words," echoed from long ago.

Suddenly Tomanto exploded, "Lundy, you and I need to ride our horses in the valley. Teena will pitch camp with us and prepare all the fish we can eat." To himself he vowed, *When we ride in the valley, and camp under the starlit sky, then I will tell you how I found Truth among your people. I will tell you how I have peace in knowing that God is the God of the universe, and His son, Jesus, is now my Lord. I will tell you of forgiveness.*

Out loud he said, "Lundy, what a joy you are to Teena and me. Someday you, too, will have sons who will ride the offspring from Desert Wind and my stallion, Big Chief."

Outside the plane, the sky darkened, the stars coming out one by one. The passengers on board were quietly settling down with pillows tucked under their heads.

Kips closed his eyes, thankful for the lifting of clouds from Lundy's mind. He couldn't sleep, but seemed to hear the roll of the ocean, the cry of sea gulls, and the warm breeze sighing through the dune grasses. He could see Rebecca running on the beach, her golden hair in the sun.

Beside him, Lundy slept soundly, his boyish face relaxed. Tomanto couldn't know that as Lundy slept, he dreamed of Desert Wind in the valley and riding toward him came the golden-haired Rebecca Cranston on a young Arabian mare.

twenty-eight

Abigail Thornton

Abigail Thornton sat on the east patio, where the sun's warmth eased the aching of her weary body. White hair framed her classical features where deep, determined facial lines had been etched by her strong will.

The old servants were gone, and she had difficulty teaching the new staff how to run the Thornton household efficiently. *Why did servants grow old and retire when they were needed the most?* she wondered bitterly. *Teena and Kips on the reservation. Meggie ill in a nursing home. And my only child, Helen, in Europe — only God knows where, or what she and that Italian designer are doing.*

She missed Nelson Lundstrom. He had seemed so strong and dependable. Somehow she knew that her daughter had destroyed him. Even Edward Thornton, her husband, had failed her — died when she needed him the most. But, Lundy was back in Arizona. Oh Lundy! I have plans for you!

With a twinge of regret, she remembered how she ignored this lonely child, turning him over to Tomanto and Teena — glad at the time to be free of him. Like her daughter had been.

Somewhere in her memory she recalled Tomanto coming into her household many years ago. There was that big argument about an Indian attending the same university that her husband, Edward, attended. It was that impossible old man, Edward's father, who insisted that Tomanto be treated as an equal. But Abigail quickly took care of that; Tomanto was kept as a servant.

But then, did she win? Her husband, Edward, was dead. Tomanto was an acclaimed artist. And worse, she had no servants like Tomanto and Teena.

But now there was Lundy! No one had previously out-maneuvered her and she knew how to use persuasive powers to pressure Lundy to take care of the Thornton affairs. After all, his father had been persuaded by Helen.

Abigail was determined to arrange a good marriage. "Money needs to marry money." She spoke out loud to herself. Within moments Abigail Thornton reached for the telephone and the social event of the season was in the making. Her eyes glistened with excitement.

She knew just the girl for Lundy! Marilyn Morgan, the beautiful, vivacious daughter of the family physician, Dr. Paul Morgan!

Abigail remembered how Paul Morgan, the young doctor from a prominent family in town became their family physician. When Abigail's own doctor retired, the young cardiologist took his place and became the Thornton's doctor.

Helen and the new Dr. Morgan moved in the same social circles. Abigail had secretly hoped that Helen would be interested in the handsome doctor. Instead, she eloped with the blond Nordic, Nelson Lundstrom from North Carolina — definitely not on the social register. The Morgan name was synonomous with wealth and social prestige. But then, Helen always had her way, especially with her father.

Now there was no Thornton to inherit the vast Thornton enterprises. She was sure that Helen had refused to have children, just as she herself had refused to have more than one child. Lundy Lundstrom, Helen's stepson, would be the only heir when Helen died.

"I should have been more gracious to the child," she thought out loud, "but I still have power, and time is running out for all of us." She was confident that Marilyn Morgan and young Lund Lundstrom would make the social headlines. Lund's father had developed the Thornton Enterprises into a powerful financial empire. Edward Thornton trusted and respected his son-in-law, and surely Lund would follow in his father's dimension.

Did it matter that young Lund had little desire for the world of finance? Let him taste its power and Lund Lundstrom would be caught in its iron-fisted grasp. But it would take a beautiful, seductive young woman like Marilyn to hold him. Marilyn knew the power of wealth.

Her father, Dr. Paul Morgan, had indulged her every wish, just like Edward Thornton had yielded to Helen's whims.

Abigail smiled to herself at the story of Marilyn's grandfather, Adrian Morgan, a confirmed bachelor who shocked the social world by eloping with a beautiful young woman — a servant girl in the old Thornton household.

The comments, "Old enough to be her father," changed to, "Have you ever seen such a devoted husband and father." Adrian Morgan lived to see his son Paul graduate from medical school. It was after Adrian's death that the young Paul Morgan set up practice in Arizona. Later he married a prominent socialite. Two years later Marilyn was born.

Abigail watched the winsome Marilyn charm her way through life. Her father was admired and respected by everyone, but especially by Abigail's husband, Edward Thornton. They would sit by the open fire and talk for hours, discussing world affairs and their favorite hobby, fishing.

Medicine and the world of finance would be forgotten when the two men, the one older, and the other younger, would pack up their fishing gear and take off to the mountain streams.

Teena would prepare a lunch and Tomanto would pack the gear into the car, then stand quietly by and watch them drive away.

The late Nelson Lundstrom was deeply respected by Edward Thornton and they worked well together in the business world. But when it came to Edward Thornton's private world, the door was closed to everyone but the doctor.

Stories and laughter emerged from those carefully planned leisure hours. At times Marilyn would accompany her father, and climb up in Edward Thornton's lap and charm him — just as Helen had done as a child. Abigail watched the two with envy.

In the midst of her reverie, Abigail thought *Yes, Marilyn would be just the one for young Lund. Strange how the past comes into focus when one gets older!* "But before the party that horrible painting in the library must come down," she announced to the empty room. "Why Edward wanted that Indian Chief I'll never know. Since Lund admires it, I'll give it to him — soften him up a bit," Abigail smiled to herself. Her mental plans continued.

Lund would be home any day from his two-week camping trip with Tomanto. What on earth could anyone do in the valley — riding horses and fishing? It was that Indian, Tomanto. She would get Lund away from him and Teena. It was time young Lund faced reality as to his social position. He owed that much to the Thorntons.

October would be a good time for the social debut of Lund Lundstrom, her self-appointed grandson. Other parties would follow and Lund would be a popular young man. She would see to that. Besides she needed someone to oversee her affairs since Helen was cavorting around Europe with Roberto. She would have to plan carefully, without Tomanto's knowledge.

Abigail decided to start her invitations with Marilyn Morgan. Yes, this would be a gala season that no one could forget.

* * *

Within a few days Lundy returned from his camping trip. He was seriously considering moving back to North Carolina. He would have to tell Abigail Thornton at once. Then, when all the business affairs had been settled, he would travel with Tomanto to the art showings, then visit Teena and the reservation once again. He would be interested in the progress of Tomanto's building plans. Teena's dreams were being realized. Lundy felt a pang of loneliness. He had no dreams. Perhaps on Wrightsville Beach. . .

The final plan would include the breeding of Desert Wind by Tomanto's stallion, Big Chief. Then he could transport his Arabian mare to North Carolina. He would keep the condominium in the Thornton Villa, where he could return for visits.

Reluctantly he entered the Lundstrom house to sort out his father's personal possessions. He packed them carefully in the trunk. When he picked up Melissa's Bible, he held it with quiet reverence. This was his mother's Bible — the mother he never knew. *Why did she have to die?* he grieved quietly. In the front of her Bible she had written: Forgive our trespasses as we forgive those who trespass against us.

Once again Lundy remembered the final days with his father. "Forgive Helen, Lundy-Boy, as God forgives us." Lundy buried his head in his arms as he knelt beside the trunk. "I can't, Dad, I can't. I miss you more than ever. I feel so alone. Teena and Kips are caught up in their dreams for the reservation. I have no plans, just a longing to belong someplace. Oh, Dad, I don't know where I belong, and I feel so numb with hate for Helen. She took you from me, and me away from the only home I ever knew — Noragram and Big Lund. Help me, Dad!"

As he stood to leave the room, Lundy looked long at the painting of the "Boy and the Sea." He wept for the childhood he had lost. In the corner of the painting he found a poem. His father must have written it.

> You can't go home again,
> No looking back;
> Ahead the shaded glen
> Or sunlit track;
> Beyond the woods and sky,
> The ocean shore,
> For time is fleeing by;
> Closed is the door.
>
> You can't go home again
> To childhood days
> Of sailing ships and then
> Pull back from waves

That beat too high and fast;
The tie won't hold
For childhood's boats are past,
The sea is bold.

You can't go home again
Except in dreams,
The flowers were blooming then;
Now it seems
The vines have overgrown
Each budding thing;
All the beauties known
Have taken wing.

You can't go home again.
The fireplace bare —
Sweet memories when
Dreams were there
Beside the open hearth
When day was done,
Home filled with love and mirth,
Now they are gone.

You can't go home again,
Old homeplace sold.
Tall trees in sorrow bend,
The wind is cold;
Inside the embers charred;
A broken lock,
The swinging gate is barred,
Stand still, oh clock.

You can't go home again.
Across the hill
The cloud is filled with rain,
The air is chill.
So sleep in peace my love
In churchyard green;
We'll all be home again
When faith is seen.

He picked up his mother's Bible again and turned to the Gospels. "Let not your heart be troubled, ye believe in God, believe also in me," he read. For a moment there was a glimmer of light, then bitterness closed the door binding him to the dark night of his soul.

Lundy closed the door and returned to his suite at the Thornton house. The desert winds swept leaves across his path. Ominous clouds hid the moon.

twenty-nine

The Party

Abigail Thornton's invitation to join her for dinner set the stage for her carefully directed questions about North Carolina. When she sensed Lundy's loss of direction for the future, she quietly suggested a waiting period. "You must be certain about moving back to Wrightsville Beach, Lundy. You've spent most of your life here in Arizona."

She acknowledged her regret at not spending time with him as a child and voiced her admiration for his father. With beseeching eyes, she asked him for help in her social plans. "A beautiful young lady needs an escort for my fall party. You will forgive and humor an old lady, won't you? After all, I have no one."

She seemed so frail and helpless while her eyes begged for an answer.

Lundy's uneasiness encouraged Abigail. "Why, you are the most handsome bachelor around. You will say yes — you will stay on and make my party a success? I really need your help!"

Lundy couldn't refuse. After all, a few weeks more or less couldn't make much difference in his plans.

Abigail Thornton was ecstatic!

Lundy had planned to go to his father's office to pack his personal items for North Carolina. Those plans could wait. He remembered the sense of awe he felt when Kips first took him to his father's suite. He sat in the leather chair and looked out over the city, feeling small and frightened. His father seemed like a stranger. Lundy had begged to go home with Kips.

"Such a long time ago," he mused to himself, "and I still want to go home to Kips. This world is not my world. I guess I feel the pull of the sea from my Viking forefathers. But for now, even North Carolina can wait.

The weeks passed quickly and the night came when the lights in the Thornton mansion blazed across the spacious grounds. The orchestra sent the sound of music into the autumn night. Servants in starched uniforms greeted the guests and ushered them into a room filled with candlelight and flowers.

Abigail, in a royal-blue evening gown, stood beside Lundy and Marilyn Morgan, greeting her guests. Once again, she was the charming hostess of the yesterdays when the mansion was filled with music and laughter. Tonight she stood with Lundy to let all the social world know that her self-appointed grandson was a man of destiny.

Marilyn Morgan's black hair framed a perfectly oval face. Deep-set brown eyes, soft, limpid pools of night, sparkled and shimmered like her soft cranberry silk gown. She knew her power, and turned seductively to greet the guests.

Lundy felt at ease with Marilyn. She kept a running conversation with bubbling humor and wit. She knew everyone, and she managed to maneuver Lundy through the happy guests with brief introductions.

Across the room Lundy saw Marilyn's father, Paul Morgan, and made a special effort to thank him for caring for his father.

"I liked your father, Lund," the doctor said. "I kept hoping for a complete recovery. I think we might have been good friends if we had known each other longer. No one realizes how difficult it is to lose a friend — and a patient — especially a man still in his prime. I lost my best friend when Edward Thornton died. He was like a father to me, besides a real friend and companion. I miss him." Morgan looked up. "But, my young man, we are at a party and I see two beautiful women coming in our direction. Lund, I want you to meet my wife, Marlene — and you already know my princess, Marilyn."

He looked tenderly at his wife. "I hear music for waltzing, Marlene." Bowing low, "Mrs. Morgan, may I have the pleasure of this dance?" Laughingly, they waltzed out of sight.

Before Lund realized it, he was holding Marilyn in his arms, dancing to Wayne King's "The Waltz You Saved for Me" — a favorite of the older generation. When the tempo changed, the two moved in perfect rhythm. Lundy was lured into a daring mood. He was surprised that he could forget the past in the adventure of the present.

Music and champagne flowed together and the night was soft and warm. Marilyn made him feel alive.

"What a night to remember!" one guest exclaimed.

"No one gives a party like you, Abigail!" Marlene Morgan assured her.

"What a handsome couple!"

"Where have you been hiding that handsome Lund Lundstrom, Abigail?"

"He'll be the catch of the season!"

Abigail smiled to herself. Marilyn knew how to handle a man. She glanced out on the patio and saw Marilyn in Lundy's arms. He held her close and Marilyn tilted her lips toward him. Time stood still for Lund Lundstrom.

Before Lundy realized it, he accepted a dinner invitation from Marilyn's mother. "Yes, I could delay my plans for a few weeks."

Suddenly there were parties, luncheons, dinners. There were always special people to meet, political and social functions to attend. Teena, Tomanto and Noragram faded into the distant past. The urgency of the present grew increasingly demanding.

Telephone calls and notes to North Carolina offered excuses for the delays. There seemed to be no stopping place. Events controlled him, but a least he felt alive for the first time in his life. Handling the business affairs for Abigail made him feel needed.

Marilyn's family were delightful people, especially her grandmother Maude who had recently come to live with the Morgans. Maude avoided all the social life but enjoyed her gardens in the summer and a warm fire on cool nights. Books and music were her companions, and she kept a journal of poems that she had written through the years. Her eyes seemed dull, far away, but she enjoyed hearing the stories about the parties, especially at the Thornton house.

Maude spoke tenderly about her husband, Adrian, and his kindness and devotion to her. Her face glowed when she spoke of her son Paul, the delight of her life. "He is a fine doctor, Lundy, and I am so proud of him. He could have been a spoiled rich man's son, for Adrian Morgan gave him everything, but he gave him more than wealth. He taught him wisdom and a desire to be a service to humanity. I am especially proud of Paul.

"I'm afraid his wife Marlene loves the social life more than he does. As for their daughter Marilyn — Paul adores her and, I'm afraid, spoils her. She needs a strong young man like you, Lund."

Lund smiled and patted Maude's hand affectionately. "You remind me of my grandmother," he added softly. Then he said, "Your son, Paul, cared for my father in his final illness. I am deeply thankful to Dr. Morgan."

"Yes, I heard that," Mrs. Morgan continued. "He also cared for Edward Thornton, but he was too late. He died alone. She grew quiet and thoughtful. "The days and years go swiftly, like a tale that is told. Love alone endures forever."

Days blended into weeks. Lundy and Marilyn attended the Arabian Horse shows, visited art galleries, even rode horses in the valley. Marilyn's charm was transforming the reserved Lund Lundstrom into a dashing bachelor who was the envy of debutantes of the social events. The hurts of the past were dulled by the adventures of the present. The notes and phone calls to Noragram continued with excuses for the delay in returning to North Carolina.

Then one day Tomanto appeared at the Thornton estate. Abigail Thornton received her old servant with cool restraint.

"No, Lundy is not here. I do not know when he will return."

Tomanto went to the cottage to wait. In his hand he held the society page with pictures of Marilyn and Lundy. Tomanto grieved quietly — and prayed.

thirty

The Choice

Marilyn and Lundy sat in front of the open fireplace in the Morgan library. Dr. and Mrs. Morgan had taken grandmother Maude to visit old friends in another town. The house was quiet, except for the crackling fire. It had been a long day of Christmas shopping, then an evening of dinner and dancing.

When Lundy stood to say good night, Marilyn pulled him gently to her. "Oh, you don't have to go. We are all alone tonight." Marilyn's arms encircled his neck and her warm lips coaxed teasingly.

Lundy drew her soft body closer to him and the strapless evening dress slid softly to the floor. Lundy threw his jacket and tie across the room as they blended into the luxurious comfort of the sofa beside the fire.

A passion raged within him. He was alive! In his arms was a beautiful woman, and he reached for her with a cry of pain. All the hurt of childhood, the unfulfilled love of youth and hate for Helen burned together in a raging fire. Only the responsive passion from the girl in his arms could release the longings in his soul. Perhaps then he could be free — free to live and love.

He responded to Marilyn's hungry kisses and groaned in his need for her. All his pent-up longings crashed about him like the waves on the ocean's shore.

Before yielding her body to him, Marilyn murmured, "Let's get married before Christmas and Abigail Thornton will make us her sole heir. She has great plans for us."

Lundy was powerless on the tide of passion. Rising out of the mist he saw Helen's face, and hate possessed him. He reached for Marilyn with greater desire.

Then into his heart came the words of Tomanto, "Hate and lust can live together, but true love lives with forgiveness." With the words came the yearning for love. This was not love. Suddenly, Lundy pushed away; he was breathing hard. With an unknown source of strength, Lundy released the sensual form of Marilyn Morgan.

"No, Marilyn, " he said, his voice husky. "We are not ready for marriage or love, for I have too much bitterness in me, and you, beautiful girl, hunger for power. Abigail Thornton will not control my life. Don't let her control yours!"

Marilyn's passion turned to fury. She grabbed her gown and held it in front of her. "Go ahead," she screamed, "Run to North Carolina, but Abigail Thornton won't leave her fortune to you."

Lundy gripped her shoulders and held her firmly. "You don't understand, Marilyn. I don't want more power. My father sold his soul for passion and power and I almost did the same. You don't need more wealth, Marilyn. You, too, need to love and be loved."

"You are a moralist, Lundy. You can have it all — power and pleasure — and you can have it whenever and wherever you want it. I intend to live life to the fullest, with or without you. No one can hold me!"

Lundy saw the same cold fury in her eyes that he had seen i Helen. Tonight he understood what had happened to his father, and he loved him with genuine compassion. "I'm sorry, Marilyn, but I am not the one for you."

"Coward," she stammered. "Are you a man or aren't you?"

"Man enough not to use you." He looked steadily at her.

"Marilyn, please listen to your grandmother. She has much wisdom and understanding, and knows the meaning of love. Trust her and don't be manipulated by Abigail Thornton." He cupped her face gently in his hands. "And don't let men manipulate you. You're too beautiful — too worthwhile."

As he picked up his jacket and tie, Lundy felt the surge of passion wash out of his body, like the waves washing back to the ocean. Slowly, like an early sunrise, he sensed warmth and light enter his soul. He slipped his jacket around Marilyn's bare shoulders and held the beautiful girl with a new tenderness. "Marilyn, you and I almost went to the place of no return tonight. Please forgive me?"

"What stopped you?" she asked bitterly.

"Kips's words of wisdom came to me, like soft spring rain on the hot dusty desert: 'Love cannot live with hate. Only the passion of lust can join the power of hate.'"

"Go, Lundy. Please go. Don't make a bigger fool of me by staying, lecturing me."

"Marilyn, don't turn away; listen to me. I am a moralist, because I saw the old-fashioned love between Teena and Kips. I was reminded of my mother's love for my father. When my mother was killed, bitterness and hate engulfed Dad. Then Helen Thornton came along. Helen's passion was no substitute for love."

Suddenly Marilyn leaned against him, crying softly.

"Before my father died," Lundy said softly, "he forgave Helen, and went home peacefully. Marilyn, when that happened I vowed to hate my stepmother and get revenge. Tonight — here — I understood the power of unforgiveness. I would have destroyed you, hurt you to get even with Helen. Love is giving. Passion takes and is destructive. I almost took your beautiful body tonight, not because of love, but to use you to meet my need. That is wrong!"

"Planning for the priesthood, my celibate Lund?" Marilyn's words pierced like a dagger.

"A man rises or falls in his own will, Marilyn. We rivet our chains by habit. When I marry, it will be for love, for a lifetime."

Marilyn grew quiet. The tears fell like a gentle rain after a storm.

"Lundy, I've never been with anyone before. My friends had many affairs. Some had abortions. You are right about my grandmother. She has spoken of love and passion. Because of her I did my share of teasing, but it was all an act — that is, until you came, Lundy. That was not an act."

"I know."

"But did you know that Abigail Thornton planned all of this — every move? I went along, like a game of conquest. Abigail promised to leave us a fortune if I could settle you into the Thornton power play by Christmas."

Lundy walked over to the fireplace and put his head in his hands on the mantle. "All the pieces are coming together like a giant puzzle. What a fool I have been, and to think I despised what Dad and Helen did. I almost did the same!"

Slowly he turned back to Marilyn. "Thank you for your honesty. You brought life and feeling into me, and for that I am grateful. To me, you are a precious friend, more dear than before. Someday, there will be someone special in your life, someone you can love and respect." He touched her cheek. "Please, can we still be friends?"

Marilyn wept quietly. The storm had moved out to sea, gone from both of them.

It was three in the morning when Lundy pulled into the Thornton driveway. Dark clouds moved across the sky, making a path for a new day. A light was burning in the white cottage.

Tomanto stood in the doorway watching the crimson glow across the morning sky. Lundy stopped, startled, then with a cry of joy, Lundy flew to his old friend.

"I'm going home, Kips. I'm going home for Christmas!"

thirty-one

The Passing Storm

Rebecca Cranston's heart skipped a beat when she saw Lundy's lean form round the dunes toward Nora's kitchen. Nora's country ham and grits sent signals to the early morning jogger that breakfast was ready.

Standing discreetly behind her window's ruffled curtains, Rebecca watched pensively. Lundy was home in body, but it didn't seem enough.

She knew that Nora was troubled also, for she saw her take her dog Bowser for an early walk to the favorite trysting place, an old log by the dunes. There Nora talked out loud to God and Big Lund, the old shepherd dog a silent listener. They missed Big Lund.

The night before, Nora and the dog had watched the last of the storm when the angry ocean reclaimed a part of the berm.

Funny, Rebecca thought, *how Nora seems to know when a storm is coming. How many times has she said, "Tomorrow the sun will shine, but first comes the wind"?* Today the storm had passed; the sun was shining, breaking through the winter-gray sky.

Lundy had been gone for two hours. *Is he taking a long journey into the past?* Rebecca wondered. *Will it bring meaning to the present?* She would wait. If only Tomanto were here! But now it was the Christmas season and there was much to do. Her gift for Lundy was tucked away in a chest.

Tomorrow she would suggest a shopping trip, but this day belonged to Nora. Sunday, they would all be in church and then home for the Cranston's Sunday dinner. She would wear her new dress and let her long hair be windblown and free.

When they heard that Lundy was coming home for Christmas, she had helped Nora get all the decorations out of the attic. Big Lund had loved Christmas, but since his death Nora hadn't had the heart to decorate the Big House. She spent most of the holidays with the Cranstons. Now, with Lundy home, Nora wanted to decorate everything and put lights outside as well. *Maybe,* Rebecca thought, *they'll invite me to help trim the tree.*

The next day, Rebecca took Lundy to the Cotton Exchange where they visited the small shops, ate ice cream at the Scoop and nibbled on fudge. Together they strolled along the river front park and toured the U.S.S. North Carolina. While eating lunch at the Pilot House, they watched the boats on Cape Fear River.

Lundy selected Christmas gifts for all the family as Rebecca took him through the new Independence Mall and the historic district of the old seaport city. The restoration of Wilmington intrigued Lundy.

On one particularly cold evening, they took a long walk on the beach, huddled together against the winter winds. Rebecca spoke of her future plans to attend the university and major in special education. "I want to help problem children to learn, Lundy. I've been so blessed with a loving family, and I want to give that kind of love and understanding to children who aren't as fortunate." She added softly, "To whom much is given, much is required."

Lundy looked at Rebecca with an expression of awe. "You

are grown up, aren't you? Just seventeen and you know exactly what you want to do. Look at me, I'm twenty-four now and I still don't know." He took her hand.

They walked in silence while the ocean's roll mingled with their thoughts. Finally he said, "I'm home, home with my adoring grandmother. I know she needs me, but, Rebecca, I feel so purposeless. I have every tangible thing a man could desire but I need a dream. A man is dead without a dream."

"Your dream will come, Lundy. Just take one day at a time. Your healing will come slowly but it will come. Then you will know the purpose for which you were born." She looked up at him. "God has a plan for every man, Lundy, and you will know. You will know."

He laughed. "You sound like a preacher, Little One."

"I grew up in a parsonage, remember?" She wanted to shout out, "I love you, Lundy Lundstrom. I have always loved you, even as a child in my make-believe world." But she was afraid to reveal how deeply she felt. Would he laugh? Would he believe her?

"I think I came home to Wrightsville Beach to find myself. To find my dream."

"You'll find it, Lundy. You'll find God's plan for you. Just as the tide ebbs and flows, there is a season for everything. For now I think the joy of home and family is enough to enjoy. It's Christmas and you're making the holiday come alive again for Nora. That could be your purpose for the moment."

"Noragram seems so frail. It's as though I've just found her again and I'm afraid I'm going to lose her."

"Enjoy her for as long as you have her, Lundy. She's special to all of us. You have no idea how special she is to me. When I was a baby, she rocked me so much my father said I'd never learn to walk," Rebecca laughed. "But here I am walking with you."

With the last remark, they raced together on the beach until they rounded the dunes toward Nora's kitchen.

Nora heard them coming, stomping up the steps, laughing. "That sounds good, doesn't it, Browser?"

Browser thumped his tail and ran to greet them.

* * *

On that Sunday morning in 1981 Lundy sat quietly beside
Nora while ushers set up more chairs in the aisle for the
Sunday morning parishioners.

Nora's hands were folded, her eyes closed in prayer.

A hush fell over the congregation as Craig Cranston walked
in, the choir just behind him. From the soprano section,
Rebecca threw a quick smile in Lundy's direction. Then the
organ, piano and orchestra joined in the opening hymn: *All
hail the power of Jesus' name . . . and crown Him Lord
of all. . .*

What music! The air was electric with the joy of worship.
The church vibrated with sound. *These people love church,*
Lundy thought as he settled back for the sermon.

People were actually opening their Bibles. He didn't even
own one. He never even read one, except when he had
read to his dad from his mother's Bible.

Craig Cranston stood behind the pulpit, an open Book in
his hand. His deep blue eyes seemed to burn into Lundy's
soul. His voice was rich and clear when he said, "Isaiah
22:23 says, 'I will fasten him as a nail in a sure place.' "
He smiled at the congregation. "A fishing vessel floundered
off the rocky coast where cliffs rose above the fjords. The
boat crashed on the rocks, but the fisherman was able to
swim to the foot of the cliff. Above him was a ledge of
safety — a harbor from the pounding surf.

"The swimmer used every ounce of his strength to reach
the cliff but the waves had washed the cliff smooth as glass.
Because he found no place to hold on to, the fisherman
was washed out to sea, only to be brought back by the
waves and dashed against the rocks.

"A minister in the fishing village heard the story and
painstakingly chiseled out steps for a place of refuge. But
the ocean's relentless tide, and time, washed the rocks
smooth again. Then another man drove iron stanchions into
the cliff and dropped a rope. Today, like that man, I will
drive four iron stanchions into the slippery cliff of life. The
atonement . . . the battle to believe . . . your choice or

chain . . . and the discipline of order."

Lundy listened intently. He heard Craig say, "There will be slippery places made by life's pounding storms but a man of wisdom begins his journey through life with his heart made steadfast in God — "

Rebecca listened intently. *Is that why she has a clear purpose of life?* Lundy wondered. *Has she made that choice to obey God? Is that why I — Lundy Lundstrom — am so purposeless? Can it be that I have a choice to make? Does this God call for action?*

After the service, Lundy slipped out a side door. Nora would ride with the Cranstons and he'd join them there a little later for Sunday dinner. But first he had to walk the beach and allow the pounding surf to master the beating of his heart.

Today he had been introduced to God. Would he open his heart to acknowledge that introduction? To make that choice? He turned his coat collar up around his neck, trying to ward off the wind. The struggle inside him was momentous, raging with hurricane force. And mixed with the storm was the question of forgiveness. Could he — would he — forgive Helen Thornton?

Helen! He clenched his fist.

thirty-two

The Restless Wind

T he stallion, Big Chief, pawed the earth, restless to race across the valley with Tomanto on his back. Tomanto's black eyes gazed into the blue Arizona sky, then off to the mountains and the tall cactus that stretched endlessly across the desert sand and rocks. He steadied the great stallion with an affectionate rub behind the ears. "I know you miss racing with Desert Wind and Lundy. So do I. But now I must feast my eyes on the beauty of the valley and store the memory in my soul."

Big Chief grew quiet under the voice and touch of his master. Silhouetted against the sky, like an old west painting, Tomanto travelled the back roads of memory. He felt a restless longing for Lundy, the only son he had never known, another man's child. He missed the long rides in the mountains, the camp fires, the opportunity to hand down his grandfather's stories.

It was as if he could see the stretch of aspen trees above the rocks and foliage and hear his grandfather's voice telling of the forgotten forest, a paradise of tall timber, bright lakes and endless prairies. His grandfather knew all the old plant species in the alpine mountain heights.

As a child, Tomanto had sat with his grandfather beside quiet pools of water lilies watching the reflection of the towering pines.

"Tomanto, my son, store the beauty of the ages into your soul and meditate on the rock formations above the canyon, rising like Indian warriors." His grandfather's words came clearly again, just as the memory came of trips with Lundy to the Sycamore Canyon, fishing for trout in the land of lakes near the small town called Williams.

Tomanto patted his horse gently and spoke out loud. "We almost made an Indian out of Lundy, Big Chief. He has been a part of the reservation, studying the art and culture of the centuries. I even took him to Tuzigoot National Monument, a pueblo of rooms terraced down to a limestone ridge." Big Chief shook his mane and pawed the sand.

Tomanto's heart ached at the memory of the child, Lundy, visiting the Grand Canyon deer farm, the Montezuma Castle, or going on picnics at the park and zoo. How much Nelson Lundstrom had missed! He recalled Lundy's excitement at the Fairfield Snowbowl where the chair ride gave a view of the San Francisco Peaks. There were concerts, art galleries, sports events.

"Big Chief, despite all our good days, there was always a loneliness in Lundy. Created things and places never replace the love of a home and family. How thankful I am that Teena and I did all we could to give that boy the love he needed."

Today, like Big Chief, Tomanto was pawing the desert sand, wanting to race into the future. He had settled with Teena on the reservation. She was content at home, with her mission complete — the recognition and success of her husband.

But Tomanto still had dreams of travel, so he could see more of the world's great art; yet, he too, was at home in his heart. Although his mind longed to reach for all the far away places, he was at home with God. He was at peace. He was a man with dreams and longings, but not beyond the will of His Creator. That made the difference.

He longed to see Lundy fulfilled, with his heart at peace and a purpose for his life. Beautiful Rebecca, the golden princess! She made him long for his youth.

"Open his heart, O Creator of the heavens, earth and sky, Creator of man. Grant Lundy the wisdom of the ages." Horse and rider sat silhouetted against the sky, the silence of peace around them. The molten moment held the past, present and future within the gentle wind.

The moment passed, and with a sigh Tomanto spurred his horse across the valley. Together they raced into the wind, horse and rider blending in rhythmic motion, while the blue skies, mountains and lakes blurred into one giant canvas.

Tomanto's thoughts raced together as he sorted the unanswered questions for Lundy in the days to come. Someday he would see Lundy again and when he did he would have to tell Lundy that Helen had returned from Europe, broken in spirit. Roberto had deserted her for a young artist with a promising career. And now Helen was alone, drinking heavily. He wondered how Lundy would react. Would Helen's need stir a sensitivity in him?

At least he would be glad to tell Lundy that Marilyn Morgan had turned her back on the social life to work with children. She had found a close companionship with her grandmother Maude. Someday she would know that her father was really the son of Edward Thornton. Marilyn's grandmother was the girl Edward Thornton loved, but he married Abigail. He would tell Lundy that Edward died never knowing he had a son and that son was his own physician, Paul Morgan. Tomanto had spent years watching Edward Thornton with Paul, his heart aching to unlock the secret as he packed their fishing gear for their trips into the mountains. Tomanto knew that those hours with his physician were Edward Thornton's happiest hours. Lundy must someday know that Helen and Abigail were cared for by Edward's only son. *Strange,* he thought, *How we rivet our chains by habits of choice.*

Back at the stable, Tomanto gently rubbed down his stallion and brought feed and water. "Tomorrow, we ride again, Big Chief, but tonight we rest."

On the way back to his house, Tomanto leaned against

the fence to watch the sun fading in the west. "Oh, God, I pray for Lundy, that he will turn to You to find true peace and forgiveness. Oh, my Father, help him to forgive Helen, for only then can he know forgiveness and find new life in Christ Jesus, God's son.

As Tomanto walked to the house where Teena was waiting, a golden glow hung across the sky as though the sun was reluctant to leave another day. Not only had a day passed, but an old year.

Tomanto turned his gaze upward. A golden lined cloud moved softly with the wind. A splash of sunset glory burst from behind the cloud. He knew that the moment held a promise for the new year.

thirty-three

The Golden Moment

Rebecca Cranston watched Lundy pull his woolen cap over his ears and brace himself against the cold winds blowing in from the ocean. Her heart ached for the lonely runner on the desolate beach. At midnight the new year would roll in. Christmas had been a time of joy for Nora. Both houses had put candle lights in each window and decorated Christmas trees. The tree limbs had hung low over brightly wrapped packages. Logs had burned in the fireplace and Nora's baking had filled her house with the tempting aroma of spices.

Rebecca smiled wistfully, remembering Nora and Wilma Newton in the kitchen. "I'll be so happy when we can move back here, Nora. Mike is getting affairs settled in Richmond so he can retire."

Nora smiled at her friend. "It will mean so much to me to have you both near again. What do folks do without friends?"

Rebecca remembered the sound of Christmas music, the friendly voices in the kitchen, and Wilma's happy news about Chad. Rebecca smiled to herself. Wilma and Nora were never happier than when they drank coffee together and relished news of an upcoming romance. Chad was getting married! Wilma couldn't tell it fast enough. They laughed and cried together.

"We were afraid Chad would never get married," Wilma said. "Then one day he was invited to New York City by a fellow Air Force officer and met a beautiful girl — Karen Lundstrom, a distant cousin of Nelson's. "It looks as though we'll have guests from New York as soon as our house is ready."

"Oh, wouldn't Big Lund enjoy this news!" Nora's joy was running over. "A spring wedding, Wilma? How exciting!"

"And what about that grandson of ours, Nora? No special girl yet?"

"There's a girl," Nora answered. "But poor Lundy doesn't know it. He does so many things with her. But he just thinks of her as his little friend. Marriage is the last thing on Lundy's mind."

"You don't mean Rebecca Cranston — isn't she a bit young?"

"Young in years perhaps," Nora replied. "But very fond of Lundy-Boy." Nora was quiet a moment, reflecting. Then she said, "God has brought us through difficult times, Wilma. We all lived such peaceful lives in our younger days, and when the storms came it seemed that we were unprepared. Yet our faith in God grew stronger each time we faced a crisis. But with Lundy — he's come through so much in his young life. And so far he hasn't really turned to God. He spends so much time alone."

"A loner, huh?" Wilma asked.

Rebecca stood at the window, listening — sharing their pain, sharing their joy, reliving Christmas all over again. It was a time to remember forever. She wondered, as she stood there, whether Lundy would ever really see her. Or would he always be a loner?

That night, after Grandma Cranston arrived, Lundy took all of them on the candlelight tour through historic Wilmington. Rebecca marvelled at his interest in the restoration of the historic port city. "If I leave the Thornton Enterprises for good, I'd like to do something with history — with the restoration of historic sites," he announced.

Each day was filled with more activity; the crowning moment was the trip to Bradley Creek. The boats in the harbor made it look like a picture postcard. Nothing could be more beautiful than the cabin cruiser — a gift from Lundy to the Cranstons. "Let's name it Carolyn," Bert and Craig Cranston announced together.

Rebecca thought about the Bible she had given Lundy, with his name in gold letters: Lund Michael Lundstrom. She remembered his wistful look when he said, "I never owned a Bible, Little One."

Will he never think of me as grown up? she wondered. She looked at the desert painting by Tomanto, Lundy's gift to her. She couldn't think of anything that would have pleased her more. But had it been a special gift? Or did he just give gifts to everyone?

Nora's gift was to be a trip to Arizona to meet Teena at the reservation. Lundy would take her in the summer or fall. But Rebecca feared that Nora might come home alone. She sighed as she watched Lundy disappear around the dunes. The beach was barren without him. "Oh, Tomanto," she cried out. "Will Lundy ever know how much I love him? Will he ever love me?"

Christmas had always been such a happy time for her but this year was different. She had sensed such a loneliness in Lundy that she also felt a searing loneliness in herself.

* * *

As he ran the dunes, Lundy was remembering the candlelight service at church on Christmas Eve with Nora and the Newtons. Beautiful Christmas carols had filled the air just as families filled every available space. He sat beside Nora, smiling up at Rebecca in the choir. She was such a lovely girl, so deep and thoughtful for someone so young, so willing to spend time with him. *The man who wins her hand someday will be a lucky man,* he thought.

After the Christmas message, the ushers lit the candles, row by row. With candles held high, the worshipers had sung: "Oh, come, let us adore Him, Christ the Lord." Lundy had been deeply moved.

Each day was special, with friends coming to visit. Tonight was the New Year's Eve communion service. He had promised Rebecca that he would go.

As he rounded the bend of the dunes, he headed toward the Big House.

* * *

Once again the music poured from the Community Church, while families sat together in the pews. Nora and Lundy sat with the Cranstons. The organ played softly and a solemn hush of expectancy fell over the congregation as Craig Cranston prepared to conduct the communion service.

Family groups knelt around the communion table and received the broken bread and the cup of wine. "This do in remembrance of Me. Take, eat, for this is My body broken for you, and this is the blood shed for the remission of sins." Lundy heard the words within the pounding of his heart. He had not forgotten the message Craig had preached at Nelson's funeral, and against the background of music he heard again his father's voice, "Forgive Helen, Lundy. Forgive us our trespasses as we forgive those who trespass against us."

Nora led the way, and he knew he had to follow. "Forgive, forgive" pounded in his heart louder than the surf and drove him out of his seat. His feet moved quietly, in step behind Nora, and when he knelt beside the table he looked into the face of Craig Cranston.

I'm ready, Lundy thought, *ready to forgive Helen.* And out loud to Craig he said, "I believe!" Then silently and with tears flooding down his checks he said, "Forgive me, Father; in Jesus name, forgive me."

He felt Craig Cranston's hand on his bowed head. When Lund looked up, Craig was offering him the bread and the wine. "Lundy, take, eat, you are forgiven. You have been made whole, in Jesus' Name."

Peace flooded over him, and Lundy knew he had come home — to God.

When the congregation rose to sing the Lord's Prayer, Lundy thought the heavens were open and his father, mother, and Big Lund were all singing along — "For Thine is the kingdom, the power and the glory forever. Amen."

thirty-four

Joy in the Morning

The sun burst forth with glory as the waves danced for joy. The seagulls called out as they dipped and soared into the blue sky. Lundy ran into the sunlight, head high, salt breezes blowing through his tousled hair.

With abandoned joy, he ran, arms outstretched to the sky. "I'm free, I'm free!" He laughed and shouted to the sky, and the waves echoed back the joy of a soul set free — free from hate, free from loneliness, free from revenge, and free from unbelief; free to believe God!

"Oh God, I thank you! Last night was a miracle, a miracle of faith."

Around the bend of the dunes he stopped. A sense of awe and reverence overwhelmed him, a desire to worship God, creator of heaven and earth. "Teach me your will, oh my God," he prayed, "And show me Your plan for my life. I give my life to You."

A sense of overwhelming love engulfed Lundy as he stood in the sun and wind early in the morning of the new year.

He remembered the faces of the people who loved him. Nora and Wilma's cheeks were wet with tears of joy. Big Mike held him close to him, like a child, "My Melissa's boy has come home."

Lundy looked out over the ocean and remembered the Cranstons. Carolyn had put her arms around him and said, "I'll be praying for you. We love you and we are here to help you."

Dr. Craig Cranston! Oh what a man! He, too, had come through doubts into the freedom of faith. "God's Word is your guide book, Lundy, and together we'll explore the depths of discovering life in God's dimension."

But it was Rebecca's face he remembered the most. He saw the tears of joy on her cheeks, but it was the look in her eyes — such an expression of love. He remembered her arms around his neck, gentle, yet so strong, just a fleeting moment, but the words so rich in meaning: "Welcome home, Lundy, welcome home." It was as though she knew he'd come!

"Oh God, I thank you. I feel like scales are coming off my eyes, my heart, even my mind. Rebecca?"

Flashes of Rebecca came before him, sitting in the sun, bare feet on a rock — Tomanto painting her. He remembered saying, "She looks like she's looking for someone," and then Tomanto's answer, "She is."

Lundy seemed to see himself and Rebecca running together on the beach, swimming, boating, shopping — she was so secure in her faith, yet, she'd never urged him. She was always there, full of joy, but with a quiet understanding.

My mother must have been like Rebecca, he thought to himself. He could hear Tomanto say, "Your mother must have been like a river, refreshing the lives she touched. That kind of loves goes with a man through his failures and into his successes. The Helens of the world come with the fire of lightning, the tempest of the sea, the excitement of a storm; but the debris washes up on the shores of life. Emptiness remains. A river flows and blesses, my Lundy-Boy. Find love like a river."

Rebecca's presence seemed to envelop him with peace; then a veil of mystery seemed to lift as if on the wings of a morning sunrise. Lundy knew he had found the woman who would love him unselfishly. He knew he loved Rebecca.

With a cry of joy, he ran against the cold wind, but the flame in his heart cried out for the heart of Rebecca. When he rounded the dunes he saw her running with the wind. Her hair was flying in the sunlight, and her arms reached out to catch the flame.

thirty-five

Teena

"Come on, Noragram. You're getting tuckered. Let's go out on the porch and sit a spell — and get a little bit closer to that ocean you love."

She peered over the top of her glasses. "I know you Lundy Lundstrom. You just want a better view of Rebecca Cranston."

"That, too," I agreed. As we eased down on the porch swing, I added, "So you think you know me, Grams?"

"Maybe better than you know yourself."

Could she be right? I wondered. Was this my land — the place where I belonged? We swayed, feeling a cool, refreshing breeze as we sat there. "There is something special about this place, Noragram," I said, relaxing.

"Better than the Thornton Enterprises in Arizona?"

I couldn't answer. Not yet. Arizona had been my home for years. I was still weighing the balance. Abigail Thornton, my dad's mother-in-law, was a powerful woman. She controlled everything she wanted — her husband, my stepmother

Helen, my dad. Did I want that power and wealth? Abigail still offered it.

Would control of the Thornton Enterprises conflict with my fledgling faith? Would that job really make me the man I wanted to be?

As if reading my thoughts, Noragram turned and squeezed my arm. "I won't push you again, Lundy. It's your decision."

"Yeah."

"Lundy, I'd love to have you here at Wrightsville Beach — but I won't be here that much longer myself." *Her lower lip trembled.* "I'll be flying away like Miss Lottie and Big Lund. But God knows what's best for you. He'll help you decide, Lundy, and whatever decision you make, it'll be the right one."

* * *

The plane dipped and soared into the sea of clouds above New Hanover airport. Tomanto's telephone message regarding Teena prompted the hasty plans. Lundy sat quietly beside Nora and spoke quietly, "I think God will let Teena live long enough for you to meet her."

Nora gazed thoughtfully out of the window. "I want, oh so much, to say a personal thank you to that beautiful Indian mother."

Lundy clasped her hand. He was returning to see Teena, perhaps for the last time. He remembered her gentle face, framed in long braids. He could almost hear her soft moccasins padding about.

But seeing Teena meant that he would also see Helen Thornton. He had much to think about, especially after the hours of Bible study with Craig Cranston. Lundy had thought the sense of forgiveness would last forever.

"It is not enough to forgive, Lundy," Craig had said, "but we must also extend grace and mercy to those we forgive. As we are filled with the riches of God's wisdom and understanding, so we reach out to touch the ones we forgive with grace and understanding."

Wasn't forgiving Helen enough? he questioned. *Must I show God's love to her, too?*

Rebecca was sitting by the window. "Are you worried, Lundy, about Teena?".

"Yes — but also about Helen. I'm not sure I want to see her."

Rebecca leaned closer. "Lundy, we'll love her together. We have to give out of the abundance that God has given to us."

Lundy looked deeply into Rebecca's eyes. "Look what love did for me." She seemed to draw away from him.

"Will you marry me if I see Helen?"

"Someday we will marry."

"When I'm godly enough?" he asked.

They sat in silence, each in a world of thought and wonder.

Then quietly, Rebecca asked, "Will I get to meet Marilyn?"

With a quick smile Lundy answered, "Not jealous are you?"

"Were you in love with her?"

"No, because I was incapable of love, with so much hate in me."

"Was she in love with you?"

"No, I don't think so, just a strange infatuation."

"Did you have many girl friends?"

Lundy broke into laughter. "I was a loner, I'm afraid. I loved horses more than people. Of course there were parties and social functions at the Thorntons, but I only did what I had to do. Tomanto used to worry about me because I eased out of social affairs.

"My life was wrapped up in outdoor action. With Tomanto as my guide, I probably have done more than most young people. At least it kept me out of romantic affairs. I just kept a love affair with Desert Wind."

Lundy took Rebecca's hand in his with deep tenderness. "You are the only one I have ever loved, and I will love you forever."

Softly Rebecca answered, "And I have loved you all my life."

"Then marry me," he begged.

"Someday, Lundy."

When the long journey came to an end, Tomanto was waiting. With a cry of joy, he gathered Rebecca and Lundy into his arms and pronounced a blessing on the two he loved so dearly.

Nora stroked the brown wrinkled face as he held her to himself. "You are come, grandmother, in time to see my Teena."

The majestic sun marched over the mountains to announce a new day to the world. While Tomanto's car sped over the roads, Nora and Rebecca gasped in wonder at the mountains, valleys, cactus, flowers and waterfalls around them. Rocks loomed like castles and caught the rays of the sun in a myriad of color.

Tomanto pointed ahead to the Hopi Reservation with visible pride — pride in the buildings, their students and their art. Then he led them into his tiny home.

Teena was sitting up, propped with pillows. Her long braids, now streaked with gray, hung over her Indian dress, the dress of a princess, and her dark eyes searched for her beloved son. Then she reached her trembling hands to him. "Lundy."

Nora's eyes filled with tears as she held Teena in her arms. "How I have longed for this day, to say thank you."

Teena smiled, "I, too, longed for this day when the two mothers who loved Lundy would meet. He turned out pretty good, eh?" Teena chuckled, her voice raspy.

"Is this Rebecca, the heart's love? Oh yes, I can see this is the love like a river. Teena held Rebecca's hand, "Ah, when we are alone, I will tell you stories. He could ride like the wind — a true Indian. I named him Little Wind." Teena chuckled with delight. "He cried in my lap, but he never let anyone but Teena see him cry. My Tomanto taught him everything. Little Wind was our life."

Lundy knelt beside her. "Dear Teena," he cried.

"My Lundy comes to bid farewell. No, no, don't cry, not farewell forever, Tomanto tells me of the love of the Great Spirit for even Teena. Shh . . ." She raised her hand for silence. "My work is finished. Tomanto is famous and must travel while there is time, before he, too, will join me in the great sky. He says we will meet again."

Teena reached for Tomanto's hand. "We have our son, Tomanto. We have our son."

"Oh, never have I spoken so many words, but my heart is so full of the love and joy from the Great Spirit. Today I have strength to speak. My eyes have seen you, dear grandmother. My heart has heard Truth, my young friends. Once again I hold my child close to me, now a man. I, too, have seen the love of his heart, Rebecca. You have all come to me, to fill my heart with much joy and great honor. Soon I will go from this valley. Will you come to me again? You will not let me be alone? I have lived for my dream. Now I must go to the Great Spirit soon."

She leaned against her pillows, her face weary, drawn. "You will come back to me tomorrow, my son, when I am not so tired."

Lundy leaned down and kissed her. "Nothing could keep me from you, Teena."

"Come," Tomanto urged, "I will take you now to Lundy's condominium where servants have prepared a meal for you." As they drove along, he said, "We'll see Helen later." Tomanto's voice was very sad. "She is like broken driftwood cast up on the shore of life. Meggie has also asked to see you, Lundy — old and alone in a nursing home. As for Marilyn," Tomanto's smile was directed to Rebecca, "you wouldn't know her. She attends a Bible study class, much to the dismay of her mother, and then teaches handicapped children — much to the pride of her father. She refuses the social circuit — to the delight of her grandmother. She says she'll never marry."

"Someone will change that someday," Lundy said. "But, Kips, what about Abigail?"

"Oh yes, Abigail Thornton lives alone in the mansion, changing servants all the time. No one can stand to work for her. Twice a year she has her big parties and that is what Abigail Thornton lives for."

The breathtaking beauty of Lundy's condominium brought exclamations of wonder from the gentle people of Wrightsville Beach.

Brick paths circled around formal gardens and patios. In the background a marble swimming pool glistened in the sun. Tennis courts were empty.

Mountains and sky seemed within easy reach, while clouds moved lazily above gardens of flowers. The expanse of glass walls and stone patios took Nora's breath.

Treasures from a past Indian culture mingled with handcrafted furniture and woven rugs. Vases and pitchers with intricate design, made from clay, told of a day that was past.

Tomanto's oil paintings hung on the walls.

The servants watched with pleasure. From every room glass doors and walls gave a view of mountains and sky, as though the created world of God moved into the home itself.

Lundy showed Nora the designs his father had made and promised to frame them for her home on the sound.

"Nelson designed all this?" Nora was overjoyed. "Oh, wouldn't Big Lund have been proud? To think that only fear of the past kept him away."

"Oh, but he came home," Tomanto added gently. "He is with Melissa and Big Lund." Tomanto looked thoughtful, "Yet, dear grandmother, through all your tears have come much joy for many of us. I might never have known the Great Spirit."

The servants smiled as they served the special Indian dishes and laughed joyously when Nora marched into the kitchen to wash dishes. "I have to write down these recipes for Wilma and Carolyn." Nora couldn't wait to share these events with her friends.

"I have to leave now," Tomanto said reluctantly, "but Lundy will bring you back to the reservation in the morning, after we all get a good night's rest. I don't like to leave Teena longer than necessary."

"Please, Tomanto," Nora said, "let me go back with you; if I won't be in the way? I want so to be alone with Teena — to thank her again for all she did for Lundy."

"Come, Nora, it will be a pleasure to have your company. It is a long journey alone."

As they drove, Nora drew from Tomanto the history of his people; the dreams and hopes for his art; the beauty of the land of sky, mountains, valleys and rivers.

The reservation came before them with the dreams built into brick and stone — Tomanto's dream of creativity.

"Teena lived for that dream," Tomanto added softly. "Now she is a true princess, with love and respect from her people. Her mission is done. She lived for my dream, wise grandmother, but does not know the love of the Great Spirit. She is willing herself to die; for her work is finished." A shadow crossed his wrinkled, leathery face. "But perhaps you. . ."

"Perhaps Teena and I can talk," she agreed.

Teena was waiting. Her wrinkled face broke into a tender smile for Tomanto, her beloved one. Her deep eyes searched Nora's face questioningly. Nora took Teena's hand gently. Tomanto left them alone but not before he heard Nora say, "I came back to talk to you of heaven."

"I will soon go to my fathers," Teena said, "but first I will see my son Lundy again." She closed her eyes and crooned an Indian lullaby — "Oh, I forget, the past seems clearer than the present. He was so young and alone. How I loved that child — a white man's child, yet, I loved him like my own, when he was good . . . and when he was bad."

"That is how the Great Spirit loves you, Teena, like His own, when you are good . . . and when you are bad."

"He loves me? I understand that He could love my Tomanto, so wise and great, but Teena? Why me? With the wicked thoughts I've had . . . I only fear the Great Spirit."

"Not fear, Teena, but love. God wants our love. God is the Great Spirit. He made the mountains and valleys, the rivers and the buffalo of long ago. The Great Spirit loves you as much as Tomanto, or Lundy, or anyone. He loves you. He loves us all. That's why He sent His Son to pay for our sin, for all our wickedness."

"This is true? You speak the truth, wise grandmother?"

"Yes, Teena, it is true. I have given my life to God because I want to tell the world that God loves each one of us. It is for all to hear."

"You speak with the sound of truth."

"That is because it is truth. The Great Spirit sent His son Jesus. Jesus is the Son of God. He died for each one. He died for you, Teena."

"Why did He have to die?"

"His Book tells us that the wages of sin is death, but the gift of God is eternal life through Jesus. It was His death that paid for our sin."

"And He did this for me?"

"Yes, Teena. And after Jesus died, He returned from death to live forever. That shows us that He really did pay for our sins and that His payment was enough. God's love is greater than our understanding. His Book says that God loved us so much that He gave His only Son, and that whoever believes in Him will also have everlasting life. That means we will live forever in heaven with Him."

"Does one have to be wise to believe? I am still a plain, simple woman."

"No, we have to believe like a child."

A sparkle came to her eyes. "Ah, like little Lundy trusted me, an Indian, to love him. He knew I would never fail him. He believed in Tomanto and me. So we believe in the Great Spirit who sent his son? Is that it?"

Nora patted Teena's cheek. "Would you like to talk to the Great Spirit, Teena?"

"Do you talk to the Great Spirit like my Tomanto speaks to Him in his loud booming voice?"

"Oh yes, often! But sometimes very softly."

"What do you say?"

"I say, 'I love You, and I thank You for sending Your son to die for my sin.' I thank Jesus, His Son, for loving me, for dying for me. Then I tell the Great Spirit that I want to live for Him, that I want to live with Him someday."

"Just like that? Like you would talk to Lundy with human tongue?"

"Yes, just like that."

Nora waited, watching. Teena seemed very tired. She closed her eyes. For a moment she was very still, her breathing shallow. Then her eyelids fluttered. She glanced at Nora, then Teena looked out toward the beloved valley and mountains and began, her voice trembling, "Great Spirit of sky, land and sea, this wise grandmother tells me You are real. I believe what I hear is truth. I, too, thank You for Your love, for I have only had fear of You." A lone tear stole down her cheek. "I thank You for giving Your

Son to pay for my wickedness. I ask You to take me to live with You in heaven. Let the words of truth fill me with Your love, and take away my fear."

Gently Nora added, "Heavenly Father, Teena comes to You, as a child . . . as simply as Lundy came to her as a child years ago. Dear Father, fill her being with Your love so she can know she belongs to You, in Jesus' Name."

They sat in a deep quiet of the soul. Softly, like a moonbeam across the water, a smile came over the sensitive, wrinkled face — "I, too, am loved by the Great Spirit. I have no fear now. Tell my Tomanto I have something to tell him."

* * *

Later Nora knelt quietly beside her bed — a little cot in the back room of Teena's home. She would never forget the love in Tomanto's eyes when he held Teena to him. "My princess, my princess, my precious princess. Now we are one in the love of the Great Spirit."

The shadows of night could not darken the joy in Nora's heart. Praise welled up within her as she joined the angelic host rejoicing at Teena's new birth.

Early in the morning, Tomanto awakened her. "Come, wise grandmother. My Teena sends for you." His eyes were wet with tears. "I have called — Lundy and Rebecca are on their way."

Teena's strength was ebbing as they spent the morning hours with her. Her hands lay limp upon the bed. Her voice was frail, faltering. Suddenly, just before noon, she opened her eyes and gazed at each one, her eyes lingering in love on Tomanto. Then she turned to Lundy and whispered, "Say that great prayer for me again, my son."

Lundy stood with holy reverence, his voice choked with emotion as he prayed:

> "Our Father, who art in heaven.
> Hallowed be thy name.
> Thy kingdom come, Thy will be done
> On earth, as it is in heaven.

Give us this day our daily bread.
And forgive us our debts as we forgive our
debtors.
And lead us not into temptation,
But deliver us from evil
For thine is the kingdom
And the power
And the glory
Forever and ever — Amen."

When Lundy opened his eyes, Teena sat with folded hands. Moments later a cloud passed over the sun. Teena's spirit was riding on the wind — to the Great Spirit.

thirty-six

Miss Helen

Two mansions loomed against the sky as Lundy turned into the winding driveway to the Lundstrom and Thornton homes.

Behind the Thornton mansion a beautiful white cottage, Teena and Tomanto's old home, stood empty. Tonight Tomanto would return to his cottage alone.

The days had passed. Lundy had assisted the chaplain in the funeral service for Teena. He ached with pain when he remembered the cry of mourning from Tomanto.

He had watched him as he faced the mountain that lonely night and heard the old Indian mourning song. The cry seemed to wing into the night. Then he watched Nora go from the house to stand beside Tomanto. After a while they began to sing quietly, softly at first, then gaining in power:

> Praise be to the Father,
> Praise be to the Son. . ."
> Praise be to the Spirit.
> The godhead, three in one.

The godhead, three in one.
Hallelujah! Hallelujah! Hallelujah!

Lundy turned to Rebecca. "I have much to learn. I couldn't believe the change from the plaintive mourning song, from the heart of a lonely man for his mate; yet deep within the spirit of the man, in the God part of Tomanto, I heard the crescendo of praise."

"That is the song of the Lord," Rebecca answered gently. "It is the song of faith. You are learning, my love."

"As I listened, I was filled with unbelievable peace, and the sting of death was gone. Noragram has a special quality about her Rebecca, reaching out to others."

Now, as the car pulled up before the columned porch, Rebecca gasped in wonder. "You really lived here?"

"I really lived in three houses," Lundy laughed, "but the one I loved the most was Teena's cottage. I even had my dog and cat there. Their gardens were beautiful, and just beyond are the stables and pasture. I can't wait to ride Desert Wind. Tomanto will find a good horse for you.

"Abigail Thornton lives here alone, and we'll try to see her first; but if she's angry with me, she might refuse to see me. Then we'll go to my father's house, where Helen lives alone with servants."

It seemed strange to Lundy to ring the doorbell, when this place had been home for so many years. A butler, dressed in white, answered. "Please inform Mrs. Thornton that Lund Lundstrom is here."

Rebecca held Lundy's hand. It was as cold as her own.

When the butler returned, he said, "I regret to inform you that Mrs. Thornton is unable to see you."

Lundy winced. "I see, I guess that means she won't see me. Thank you." To Rebecca he added. "We will try again, later."

They walked hand in hand past the gardens and patios.

"I used to sail my boat in that swimming pool." Lundy seemed to talk to himself. "That's the patio where I saw Helen in Roberto's arms." He felt a tension rising up, like the old hate returning; and then remembered the song of faith rising out of the storms of life.

Rebecca quietly prayed.

Tomanto emerged from his cottage and the three moved toward the stone steps leading to the massive carved door of wood and brass. A slovenly maid answered, "What do you want?" She stopped when she saw Tomanto and reluctantly invited them in.

Helen Thornton was alone in the library surrounded by empty liquor bottles and ash trays filled with cigarette butts. The television blared. No one was listening.

A gasp came from Lundy! Not Helen! This dishevelled woman in a soiled robe, stained with liquor!

Tears stung his eyes, as Helen barely looked up.

Tomanto remained expressionless; only his eyes held a deep sadness. Gently he took her hand in his work-worn one. "Miss Helen, it's your old Kips." He waved Lundy, Rebecca and Nora aside, but continued talking. "Remember how we used to ride the horses, Miss Helen? You were some rider! You could always twist old Kips around your little finger, and I called you my little fairy princess. You just waved your magic wand — and there was Kips."

Helen looked at him through glazed eyes. "Tomanto, my Kips? Where's Teena? Where's my daddy? Where is everyone? Where is Nels? I'm so afraid, Kips; please take me home. I'm afraid of these people. Kips, where is home?"

Lundy held his head in his hands. "To think I could hate this poor creature. My God, help her, please help her."

Helen looked around. "Who are these people, Kips?"

"It's Lundy," Kips answered, "and his family."

Lundy moved closer, "Helen, I am Lund Lundstrom, Nelson's son. We have come to take care of you. No one will hurt you." He knelt beside her.

Helen looked around wildly. "Lundy? Nelson's little boy?" She blinked, trying to focus clearly on him. "Where is Nelson? I want to go home. Why am I so afraid in this place? Are you really going to help me? Who is that girl?"

"Helen, I want you to meet Rebecca Cranston, the woman I love."

Rebecca leaned over her. Helen stared up into those innocent blue eyes. "Rebecca!" She touched Rebecca's face. "You are beautiful. I remember now. You must be Melissa,

Nelson's Melissa. She was always here in this house with us but I could never quite find her." Helen's eyes were glazed, troubled. She looked from Rebecca to Lundy, "Oh, Lundy, how I hated Melissa — but this one, she is so lovely. Yes, Lundy, you are Melissa's child. That's why I was afraid of you. I was afraid you'd take Nelson from me."

No one in the room moved. Lundy's heart pounded, so loudly that it was like the ocean surf deafening him.

Helen seemed to fall asleep, then looked up, startled. She reached for her glass on the table beside her. It tipped, crashing to the floor, the pungent smell of liquor rising up. "Lundy, I loved your father," she mumbled. "And I was so afraid that you and the memory of his Melissa would take him away from me. Nelson was the only one I ever really loved." Her voice was a pitiful wail.

Silence hung heavy in the room again for a moment, then Helen whispered, "Why did Nelson leave me, Lundy?"

Lundy glanced at Kips. The grief etched on Tomanto's face revealed the deep sorrow in his heart for the little princess of long ago and for his beloved Teena. Kips had painted Helen in her childhood. He had seen some beauty there and had captured it on canvas. *Why did I miss the beauty in Helen,* Lundy wondered. "Helen," he said gently, "let Rebecca take you to your room for a hot bath. I'll get the servants to clean up and we'll order lunch from the club."

Lundy didn't miss the sullen looks on the faces of the servants. He made a mental note to replace them with trusted people. He would ask Kips to stay on with him for awhile in the cottage. Together they would take charge, help Helen — and perhaps help Abigail Thornton if she would let them.

He remembered Craig Cranston saying, "Give my daughter a year, Lundy. Let her be certain of her love for you. It will give you time to know for sure too, Lundy, that you love my daughter for herself . . . not because she reminds you of your mother."

And now Helen had envisioned a similarity; she had called Rebecca *Melissa*. Was he following an elusive dream — was he trying to be Nelson over again, choosing someone so like Melissa?

Lundy watched Rebecca coax Helen from the chair. Rebecca's beauty and innocence gripped him. He wanted to shout out, "Craig Cranston, I do love your daughter. For herself. I'll wait for her a year, or however long it takes." But something inside him suppressed the words.

Did Craig know that Rebecca had already refused to marry him? "Not now. Not yet," she would say.

Had Craig encouraged that? Why? What was she waiting for? "Why?" he had asked several times.

Just last night she had touched his lips with her fingers. "I can't take the place of God in your life, Lundy. I don't want to stand in your way — I don't want you to choose Wrightsville Beach just for me."

He had kissed her fingertips then. "But I thought that's what you wanted."

"Lundy, these last six months . . . you're still restless. I know you're destined for greatness, and I'm just Rebecca Cranston, the girl who loves you. I just feel there are things you have to do first, things that will let you put God first in every area of your life. Then I can be a blessing to your life, an asset — not a burden."

"What things?" he demanded.

"I'm not certain. Maybe there are still fragments of your life here in Arizona. . ."

He hadn't intended to come back to Arizona. He'd already told Abigail Thornton that he couldn't come back. Wouldn't. He had advised her to have others take over the company, to look over his share of interest in Thornton Enterprises.

And he wouldn't have come back — if it hadn't been for Tomanto's frantic telephone call about Teena. "You must come, my son," Tomanto pleaded. "Your little Indian mother Teena lies dying."

The door of the library closed behind Rebecca and Helen. He could hear Rebecca urging Helen up the staircase.

Helen! Was this the fragment that Rebecca meant? Was Helen the real reason that he would not come back to Arizona? Hadn't he forgiven Helen in his heart? Must he say it to her face? Must he tell her, *Helen, I love you,* when even as he thought the words, he choked?

Inside he felt the gentle nudging of the Holy Spirit. He

felt a fresh new sense of peace welling up in him. Kips's sturdy hand gripped his shoulder. "Lundy, my son, we must help Helen before you go home to Wrightsville Beach."

Lundy nodded. "I don't know how to tell Noragram and Rebecca. I don't want to lose Rebecca."

"You won't, my son. She is a woman of great wisdom. She will understand. She is much like my beloved Teena." Tomanto's face clouded. But only for a moment. He pointed to Nora dozing in a chair. "And your wise grandmother, she will understand, too. If only Helen had had a mother like your Noragram — one who did not scorn her."

Lundy turned and faced Kips.

Was it possible that Abigail Thornton had scorned her own daughter? Had the servants lied about Helen's condition? He and Kips would get to the truth, together.

Lundy looked around his father's house. The silver and brass were tarnished, the unwashed windows framed in dusty drapes. Paintings and small antiques were missing, some broken. These treasures from around the world, so prized by Helen! "How fleeting it all is!" he said aloud to Kips. "And how empty this house is without my father." He thought of Helen's words: "Nelson's the only one I ever loved."

An overwhelming love for this pitiful woman came over Lundy. It was more than pity. It was a reaching out, beyond forgiveness, to give her the love she had never had — not from her parents, not even from Nelson, for she had known Nelson loved Melissa.

He would try to show Helen God's love, the love that never fails — the fragment that Rebecca had mentioned.

An hour passed. Lundy walked softly from room to room, a hollow, neglected house. He turned at the sound of footsteps.

Rebecca was leading Helen by the hand. Helen was dressed in a soft blue skirt and white blouse, her beautiful black hair, now streaked with grey, was brushed into soft curls around her face. Even the long neglected fingernails were cleaned and trimmed. Make-up added color to her cheeks. A soft, gentle fragrance enveloped them both.

"You look beautiful, Helen!" In a gallant gesture, he

bowed low and kissed her hand. Helen laughed delightedly.

Her hand shook as she took the cup of tea that Lundy offered. The china cup was as fragile as Helen. "I'm so very tired," she murmured softly.

When a servant offered her medication, Tomanto said a stern "No, thank you," and took the bottle of valium.

"Miss Helen," Kips told her, "I am going to stay here, and I have sent for Dr. Morgan. A nurse is coming to stay with you until you get well. I'm also making some household changes."

She nodded, only vaguely hearing him.

After dinner, like a tired child, Helen was led to her room, where Rebecca tucked her into bed.

"Don't leave me, please don't leave me. They will hurt me, and only give me more medicine. Don't let them hurt me anymore."

"I'll stay right here, until the nurse comes and then Dr. Morgan will come to see you. Just go to sleep."

Rebecca hummed softly, some of the old gospel songs, and held Helen's hand in her own. In her heart she prayed for Helen, and thanked God for all the love that had been poured into her own life. "Please, God, help me to share with others."

By the end of the day, new servants had been employed; the old ones had been dismissed with a threat of an investigation. Tomanto reminded the departing servants that he was acquainted with every painting and priceless antique. A housecleaning crew was employed to transform the chaos into cleanliness and order.

It was almost midnight when Lundy found a moment alone with Rebecca. "Rebecca, darling, I need to. . ."

"It's all right, Lund. I already know. You must do what is best. I understand." She turned and quietly left the room so he would not see her cry.

thirty-seven

Miss Meggie

The following morning, Rebecca and Lundy left to visit Meggie in the nursing home. Nora did not accompany them. "Too much coming and going for me," she laughed.

As they drove along in Helen's car, just the two of them, Rebecca drank in the breathtaking beauty around her. She moved closer to Lundy. A deep happiness filled her.

"Will you come back to Arizona another time, Rebecca? It takes time to enjoy all the beauty in this part of the world. I'll take you to all of my favorite places."

She glanced his way and smiled. "Perhaps. Perhaps I could even be happy living here."

"When I decide where I belong?" he asked.

She nodded. "Oh, Lundy, I am deeply thankful to be a part of your road back because I know God is putting the past, present and future in His order. I know you are finding your place."

At the small nursing home on the hill, they found Miss Meggie propped up in bed, her thin, blue-veined hands clasped in despair. A look of wonder stole across her face when she realized that Lund Lundstrom had come to see her.

"I must tell you something," she began haltingly. "I told Tomanto I had to tell you the truth before I died. You see, I lied when I said there was no mail. Oh, please, forgive me? Miss Helen told me that your grandparents wanted to take you away from your father. Now Tomanto tells me that wasn't true and I had to tell you before I died."

Lundy held the frail wisp of a woman's hand. "Of course, you're forgiven. It's all forgiven, Miss Meggie. God loves you and He forgives." He looked up and beckoned Rebecca to them. "Meggie, I brought a beautiful girl to see you — hopefully, the future Rebecca Lundstrom."

She studied Rebecca. "Oh, my, but she is pretty! How kind of you to come." Then she stared at the gifts in Rebecca's hands and clapped delightedly. "You brought those for me? Flowers and a pink bed jacket?" As she took them from Rebecca, she buried her nose in the flowers. "I never had presents before," she said softly.

"You do now." Rebecca leaned down to kiss the wrinkled cheek. "Here, let's put this on right now." She slipped the bed jacket around Meggie. Then she brushed the matted hair gently, arranging it softly around her face.

"You look beautiful, Miss Meggie," Lundy said as he helped her into the wheelchair. He frowned when he noticed the threadbare robe and slippers.

Tears rolled down Meggie's cheek. "I remember the sailboat on your ninth birthday. I was afraid I'd lose my job, but I was glad you got that gift anyway."

"There were two boats that year, Meggie," Lundy said, wheeling her chair toward the doorway.

"And Miss Helen almost got one of them."

"She would have, Meggie, if Tomanto hadn't rescued it." Lundy was pushing the wheelchair down the narrow corridor, past other lonely residents. "Did Abigail Thornton put you here, Meggie?" he asked. "Oh, no. Dr. Morgan did, or I wouldn't have had any place to go. Mrs. Thornton argued with him that I wasn't her responsibility. I worked all my life — all my life. I have no one, you know. I never had a party either."

"Well, you have someone now, Meggie, and I'll see to it that you are cared for. Tomorrow I'll bring my grandmother and we will have a big party — balloons, cake and ice cream."

Rebecca hugged her to herself so Meggie couldn't see the tears. "Meggie, tomorrow we'll have Christmas and a birthday party all in one!"

"Oh, I'll never sleep tonight. I'm so excited! You have forgiven me, Lund?"

Before leaving the nursing home, Lundy requested an 8 A.M. to 4 P.M. companion who could take her for rides to the park, and if she was able, out to lunch. He would arrange the funds for Dr. Morgan to make any necessary arrangements for Miss Meggie's care and comfort.

"You're more wealthy than you've ever been, Lundy," Rebecca told him.

"Now that I am giving it away?" When she nodded he said, "Money is a cruel master, Rebecca, and the love of it damns men's souls. Money to give is a blessing. I never loved money. I learned from Tomanto that money buys power and control, but not real meaning in life. But I'm just learning how to channel it."

Rebecca touched his hand. "Only when God's love controls a man is that man free to control his wealth and plant it as seed to bless humanity."

Meggie leaned forward in her wheelchair. "Poor Mrs. Thornton sits in her lonely mansion, surrounded by wealth," she said sadly, "while her old servant here is dying alone in a nursing home."

"By tomorrow, Miss Meggie, you'll have more joy in one day than Abigail Thornton had in a lifetime," Lundy promised.

"Than we'd better be going, Lundy," Rebecca urged. "We have shopping to do, and presents to buy. I wouldn't miss this party for anything!"

Rebecca and Lundy returned home weighed down with packages and floating balloons. Nora was delighted when she saw the huge cake, with its candles, and "We love Meggie" written across it.

When the sun rose over the valley the next morning,

filling the new day with a brilliant glory, the Lundstrom household was still bursting with plans. At noon Tomanto joined Nora, Lundy and Rebecca to march under a maze of balloons, burdened down with packages, into Miss Meggie's room with a "Happy Birthday, Merry Christmas" — all at once.

Meggie's new companion had prepared her for the day's event. Lundy took pictures of Miss Meggie: one in her chair; one dressed in her soft new robe and slippers; another with roses in her lap; and several of her blowing candles and opening packages. All the lonely past seemed to melt into this one golden hour as love poured into the soul of Miss Meggie.

When the time came to leave, Nora gathered everyone around and read the twenty-third Psalm and prayed for God's blessing on Miss Meggie.

Nora looked with wonder on the face of her grandson, Lund — a reservoir of God's love. She was proud of him. A reverent silence engulfed them as though they sensed the presence of God. Even Tomanto's shadow of grief blended with the sunshine of joy for others.

For everything there is a season. Soon it would be the season for Nora and Rebecca to return to North Carolina. They wouldn't see Lundy again for almost three months.

thirty-eight

On Wings
of Glory

Noragram pushed herself up from the porch rocker and reached for her cane. "Like Miss Lottie would say, 'We've been doing a heap of talking, Lundy-Boy.' "

I stood, my lanky frame towering above her. "Thanks, Noragram."

"For what?"

"For being special. For being you."

She poked me playfully with her cane. "Go on with you. You're just like Big Lund, flattering me."

She sighed wistfully. "I wish you weren't just here on vacation — two weeks just doesn't seem long enough."

"I need to tell you something, Grams. I was going to hold off — keep it a secret until I was certain. But — it's not just a vacation."

"What then?" Her eyes brightened. "You're home to stay?"

"Not really."

"Then Rebecca? You've finally decided to marry?"

I glanced out toward the beach. Rebecca was off in the distance, strolling the whole length of the dunes, her hair blowing in the breeze — her spirit soaring even higher than the seagulls that swooped around her. "I'd marry her today if she'd go to Charleston with me on Monday."

"Charleston?" Noragram squinted. As she arched her brows, new crevices wrinkled her skin. "Charleston?" she repeated.

"I have a business appointment there."

She waited, leaning on her cane.

I glanced at my watch. "This time on Monday I'll be meeting with Bentley Harvesen. He's considering a merger with Thornton Enterprises." I let my words sink in before adding, "If the merger goes through, we'll be having a main office in Charleston to handle our contacts in Europe. Negotiations include my being assigned to the office in Charleston."

"Charleston," she said brightly, as if it were the corner drug store. "Oh, I'd love that, Lundy-Boy."

"I would, too," I admitted. "I'd be seeing you frequently."

"And seeing Rebecca Cranston."

"If I had my way, I wouldn't be coming to Wrightsville Beach to see Rebecca." I laughed at Noragram's shocked expression. "Rebecca would be with me and she wouldn't be a Cranston."

Impulsively, Noragram nudged Browser with her cane. "Do you hear that, Browser? Our Lundy is heading east for good, getting married."

"Whoa, Noragram!" I said. "If I had what I wanted . . it's just. . ."

"It's just you have some fool notion that you aren't godly enough for Rebecca."

The words sounded ridiculous when I heard them. "It's just I haven't measured up yet," I mumbled.

"Did you measure up before coming to Jesus?"

She could have hit me with a pound of wet noodles or tossed me into the Atlantic for shock treatment. Her words woke me up. "All along I've been thinking Rebecca wanted me to measure up. I guess if I took forever, I couldn't do that. Could I, Grams? I certainly haven't done much measuring up in the last three months in Arizona."

"Measuring up and salvation's the same route, Lundy. By faith, through the blood." Noragram started for the steps, then paused. "What have you been doing in Arizona?"

"Picking up the fragments," I said huskily. "The fragments that stood in the way of my marriage and my peace."

"Fragments?"

"I've been working hard at the Thornton Enterprises, negotiating for this merger. But I think my biggest success was becoming friends with Abigail and Helen. We moved Abigail into the Thornton Senior Residency, and for the first time in her life she's found real friendship with some down-to-earth, ordinary people."

"But what about her mansion?"

"Last week she decided it would make a wonderful Indian Art Museum. And guess who's in charge of the renovations?"

Grams beamed. "Tomanto. Dear Tomanto."

"He's thriving on it. If only Teena could see him."

"And Helen, your stepmother?" Noragram asked cautiously.

"Paul Morgan encouraged her to go into rehab. She'll keep her home there on the Thornton Estates. She needs that."

Noragram started down the steps. "And you, Lundy-Boy?" she asked, her words wafting on the wind.

I heard myself answer, and knew for the first time as my words followed her that my decision was sealed. "I'll keep a place there in Arizona. For vacations. For business trips. It'll always be like home for me — I spent so much time there."

She and Browser were off the porch now, heading toward the beach. Had she heard me? I wondered. "Grams," I called out. "Did you hear what I said?"

She was chuckling when she turned my way. "Of course, I heard you. I'm just hurrying out to tell Big Lund."

"Do you want me to walk with you?"

"Suit yourself," she said.

"I'll get my jogging things on and catch up with you." I went back into the house and paused for a moment at the old oak table. Grams's Bible laid there, wide open, well read — the family album beside it, closed. This was where Noragram always said good morning to God. This was where she had weathered many a storm praying for those she loved — praying for us.

Moments later I was back outside running the shortcut through the dunes toward Noragram. I slowed as I neared her. She was heading toward the inlet where Figure Eight Island stretched into the sea and the fishing boats seemed to slip into the sky. She was carrying on a conversation with the seagulls, playing a game with them, luring them with her bag of bread crumbs.

"See if you can catch this one," she called out, tossing a bread crumb in the air. A screaming gull dipped from the sky and caught the bread, mid-air. Noragram's laughter rang out across the waves. "Get on with you, now," she called to her gray friend. "The crumbs are gone. I'll be back tomorrow."

The old seagull seemed to dip a salute as he winged into the blue sky. Noragram limped on, past the sandpipers who did a dainty ballet on the shoreline. She poked the tip of her cane gently against the wriggling sand crabs as they burrowed their way into the wet sand.

They're burrowing an underwater passage to China, I thought, suddenly remembering what I had believed as a small child.

I kept following Noragram at a safe distance, close enough to hear her, but not enough to startle her. Noragram finally rested on the old oak beam that the waves had washed upon the shore so many years ago. And again I remembered my childhood when she had delighted me with stories. The driftwood had became a gallant ship washed up on shore. I was the captain shipwrecked at sea. Her stories were full of deeds of valor on deserted islands. How often we had plowed safely through the imaginary wilderness of sand dunes and grasses to raid pirate ships and to seek lost treasure. Then after munching peanut butter sandwiches with the flavor of salt spray, and drinking warm lemonade, we had gone back to Big Lund, hand in hand.

I wondered now how many times Noragram had come to this rotted old log to talk to Big Lund. Had they come together when they were alone, praying for my father and me to return home?

Browser was stretched out on the sand beside her, his head on his paws, waiting, listening. I stood behind Noragram; our faces were to the wind and the fall sun was beating on us. She patted Browser affectionately. "Some folks think

I'm talking to myself, Browser. They just don't know — exceptin' for Rebecca — how natural it is to talk to Big Lund out here. After all, we walked this beach together more that fifty years." The dog stirred. "You miss him, too, don't you, Browser?"

She rocked on the log. "Good morning, Big Lund. I'm afraid I'm a bit late this morning — it's nigh to noon. But wait till I tell you what's a happening. I've been talking with that boy of ours. All this time I've been wanting him right here at the beach with me. Now I know my thinking's been wrong. He's got a mind to do what's right. And that means going on with Thornton Enterprises. It's what he's been trained to do. But he'll be nearby. Down there in Charleston.

"Some folks have been concerned that he was choosing Rebecca Cranston because she's so much like Melissa. But I know now he turned to her because she is so alive and real and deep. Those were the things that our Nelson liked about Melissa."

I sat down in the sand, quietly, so as not to disturb her. My throat was tight but I couldn't intrude. She was somehow closer to eternity than I was. Out of the corner of my eye I caught sight of Rebecca rounding the dunes, heading our way. Still I was frozen in time, unable to stir, to run and meet her.

Browser was rubbing his head against Noragram's knee, licking her hand. Noragram was still talking to Big Lund. "Remember when I came here to talk to you about selling the house? Folks thought I ought to be nearer to town. They didn't understand that I could feel you close right here where we lived together. Everything around me is part of you. I came here to ask you what to do and then I remembered our last walk on the beach. I could hear you saying, 'The boys will come home, Nora-Girl, just wait. Nelson and Lundy-Boy will come home.' Then I knew I had to be here — I could never leave Wrightsville Beach.

"Do you know how many times, Big Lund, I wanted God to take me Home to be with Him — to be with you? But you always said God had a work and a place and a time. You said God's love would keep me safe in His care. It's true, Big Lund, I feel God so close to me and then I feel you close. Guess it's because you are there with God."

Noragram was silent for awhile, the ocean breeze blowing against her face. *Will I have her long?* I wondered. *Will she really join Big Lund soon?* Her back was to me, I couldn't see her eyes, but I was sure she was crying. "You used to tell me, 'Nora-Girl, someday Lundy-Boy will come home. Then he will need us more than when he was a child.' He did. But he's strong now, Lund. He won't need me much longer except for lovin' him. He's come to terms with God.

"But I'll go on here for awhile and keep the place so when he comes home with his wife and kids, he'll have a place to come to. What did you say, Big Lund? Oh, no. He isn't married yet. But mighty soon. But I am a little troubled about the rose bush. The bugs get to it before I do. The iris keep crowding it out. I need to thin the iris out, but Lund, you should see these gnarled fingers of mine. They can't grip anything much any more. And the palm trees — just like me, Big Lund. They got through last winter but need some trimming. Some things I don't seem to get around to doing these days. Remember the yucca bushes? Nothing stops them — winter or storms.

"Oh, my dear Lund. It's good to talk to you out loud. It helps to hear the words I'm thinking. I know some folks think I'm getting old and forgetful, but there are some things I want to forget. Then again, the past returns clearly, but I'll forget what happened yesterday."

Rebecca slipped quietly up to me, sat beside me and kissed me on the cheek. "I love you," I whispered.

She slipped her arm in mine. I grabbed her hand tightly, and nodded toward Noragram. Rebecca nestled her head on my shoulder as Noragram said, "That reminds me, Big Lund. I nigh to forgot what I came to talk to you about. You always said that Lundy-Boy would come home. He's here right now. Visiting from that fancy place in Arizona. Oh, I wish you could see him. It's like seeing our Nelson all over again — so tall and handsome. He has your walk and deep blue eyes. But then I guess you can see him." The ocean waves rolled gently. Noragram pulled herself laboriously to a standing position. She turned from her trysting place and almost tottered.

I started to get up. Rebecca held me back. "She can do it, Lundy. She's okay."

Noragram stepped around the log and gazed at us. "Well, you two," she said smiling. "You're finally together." She took a few steps toward the house, then paused. "I'm going up to the house and get us a late breakfast — sausage, grits and eggs. You come along when you're ready."

She was humming to herself as she limped away, Browser by her side.

"She knows, doesn't she Lundy?"

"Knows what?" I asked.

"That things are settled between us."

My heart pounded. "How? What? I was going to tell you . . . ask you. . ."

"About Arizona? About getting married right away?"

"How did you know?"

"I've been walking the beach all morning, praying, singing. I told the Lord it was okay, Arizona or here. As long as we could be together."

I stood and pulled Rebecca up beside me, wrapping my arms tightly around her. "There's no waiting any longer?" I asked. "You're going to marry me? Next summer? Next week?"

"*Today,* if you'd like." She turned her lips toward mine, as just beyond us the wind sang softly over the ocean.

Epilogue

Hurricane Diana

It was Tuesday morning, September 11, 1984. Television and radio stations canceled regular programs to keep the public informed about the elusive Hurricane Diana, blowing off the North Carolina coast.

Mandatory evacuation of the coastal residents was in effect. Rescue teams, emergency housing, food and water supplies were mobilized. It was the most massive, threatening hurricane since Hazel in 1954.

Nora looked out over the stormy Atlantic. Once again the angry, monstrous waves were snarling, tearing at the man-made sand dunes and cupping up the beach front. She could no longer spot the trysting log where she met with Big Lund. She spoke to the empty room, to the dog beside her. "I've lived through many storms and the sun always shines tomorrow. Come, Browser, I guess we have no choice but to go."

Browser, the offspring of Missy and King, stayed close to her heels, then barked excitedly when Craig Cranston pulled up in the truck to get them. "Carolyn went inland with the car," he said as he met Nora in the doorway. "She'll meet us at Wilma's place. Now we best hurry."

Nora was reluctant to leave. She liked to stay close by whenever the wind came up. If anything was damaged, she'd be there to oversee it!

Gently Craig assisted Nora, now eighty-two years old, down the porch steps and into the truck. "Don't fret, Nora," he said easily, trying to reassure her. "We've secured everything. Your furniture has been moved upstairs. The windows are all boarded up."

"Is the power shut off?" she asked anxiously.

"All taken care of." He ducked against the wind. "And your valuable papers and belongings are in the lock box in the back of the truck."

"Just as Big Lund would do!" Nora said softly. She looked back longingly. The Big House was almost veiled in the stormy mist. *Will the house withstand the gale?* she wondered. *Will there be looting before I get back? Will I ever see my home again? Even more important, will I ever find the log on the beach, my meeting place with Big Lund?*

When they arrived at Wilma Newton's place, the house that Big Lund had built in town, Wilma once again had everything in order. A kettle of soup simmered on the stove. A pan of cornbread was in the oven. Logs crackled in the fireplace. Carolyn Cranston had the water jugs filled and the lamps and candles in reserve.

"Seems like yesterday, Wilma." Nora stretched and hung her wet cape in the same place by the fire. A comfortable pair of slippers replaced her wet shoes.

"We'd better eat in the kitchen, never know when the power will go out." Wilma shuffled about, setting the table for four.

The winds came with a fury and the rain pelted against the boarded windows, but around the table there was a sense of peace. The soup and cornbread mingled with the conversation about the children. Craig Cranston prayed for the safety of the area, that people would be aware of God's power, as well as His love and mercy.

At 3 A.M. Wednesday, the elusive Diana, lashing to be free, seemed to be held at bay forty miles off shore. The news reported that everyone was safely evacuated from the beach area; even so, emergency shelters were set up in the schools and churches. Hospitals were on alert.

The winds and twelve-foot waves made a path of fury and destruction for the leading lady, Diana, in the pending tragedy. Still, she hovered off shore, out over the Atlantic. The people waited and prayed!

By morning there was a lull, a dismal hush, but the storm was not over. Diana was turning, churning, twirling — heading for shore again. High tides and torrential rains continued.

Then on Thursday at 3 A.M., the winds struck the coast at 125 miles per hour, pounding the surf, leveling the sand dunes, knocking out power lines in town. Nora, Wilma and the Cranstons peeked out as Hurricane Diana toppled giant oaks and towering pines. The Cape Fear River rose several feet, with five-foot waves washing down the village streets. The Coast Guard kept vigil over boats and yachts, but were powerless to prevent some from breaking from their moorings and being swept to sea.

Late that afternoon, Nora and Wilma opened the door when muddy, wet rescue workers knocked. "Yes, ma'am," the older man said, "power's out about 80 percent . . . never knew soup and cornbread could taste so good . . . looks like you prepared for an army."

Wilma laughed. "We've lived through many storms, young man," she told him.

"The sun will shine again," Nora added confidently.

"News of your coffee has gone down the line, ladies," announced one bearded young worker. "And it looks like you'll be seeing some more wet mud on your clean floor. Sorry about that."

Another worker added, "We've never seen a time like this when folks opened their homes to let us shower and get clean clothes. One restaurant has fed hundreds of workers."

Phones and power lines were out and soft candlelight brought a sense of comfort throughout the long night. They kept the battery-run radio on, turned low but loud enough to catch every news report. Tornado warnings followed the fury of the eye of Diana. Nora, Wilma and the Cranstons waited. They prayed. Gradually the sound of the wind decreased until, finally, it became less than the noise of the pelting rain.

Hours around the kitchen table and fireside brought stories of the past into the present. Craig stood, stretched his lanky legs, and stepped to the fireplace to toss another log or two on the dying embers. He coaxed and fanned the fire until a steady flame caught his serious, sensitive expression. "It's like I always tell Carolyn," he said, nodding toward his wife. "Storms bring out the best and worst in people. But God be praised, we've seen the best in our community."

Wilma rocked quietly by the fire. "It's been more than two years since your trip to Arizona, Nora. Seems like we always come back to starting places."

Nora's gaze seemed far away.

"Is something wrong?" Carolyn asked.

"I was just thinking about what Craig and Wilma said. And it's true. Lundy-Boy had to go back to the starting place, to the Thornton Estates in Arizona." Outside, nearby, they heard another tree crashing, split from its roots by the storm. Nora smiled in spite of the noise. "Lundy has been through a great many storms but it's brought out the best in him."

They sat silently, listening to the rain and the wind. Craig seemed restless. Finally, he turned to Nora and Wilma and asked, "Would you two be okay if Carolyn and I go down to one of the shelters and give a hand? I feel like we should be helping out."

"We ought to be able to handle a spell alone," Wilma answered.

"Yes, you two run along," Nora agreed. "Help out for us, too. If we went, we'd be more in the way — what with our canes and all."

We'll check the reports on the roads and the beach area while we're there," Craig said, reaching for his rain gear.

When the Cranstons left, Nora moved to the rocker beside Wilma, Mike Newton's old chair. She eased down in it, content to be alone with her old friend in a familiar setting. "Can you believe it, Wilma, thirty years since we all sat here during Hurricane Hazel — remember? Melissa and Nelson, Chad, Mike and Big Lund. Now, except for Chad, we two women are the only ones left."

Wilma pulled some books from the coffee table. "Look at these pictures, Nora — stacks of albums. We could be here all day if we start going through them." But having a "knowing" that God brings the past, present and future together, they opened the top album.

Nora and Wilma bent their snow-white heads over the open pages, while flames from the fireplace cast a glow over their wrinkled faces. They turned the pages carefully, tenderly, savoring the memories of a lifetime. Their beloved husbands. Melissa and Nelson. The smiling faces of their other children.

Chad and Karen — statined at an air base in Germany — building a snowman with their small son Michael.

Their beloved grandson Lundy — almost twenty-seven now — with his wife Rebecca. They gazed at the recent snapsots — Lundy and Rebecca on vacation at the Thornton Estates in Arizona. A picture of Lundy and Rebecca with Tomanto in front of the Indian Art Museum. And the very favorite photo of all: Lundy and Rebecca holding one-year-old *Melissa Lenora* astride Ocean Wind, the offspring of Desert Wind.

As the pages turned, so came the past on slippered feet to whisper stories from the albums — stories about the Lundstroms, the Newtons, the Cranstons. Woven into the fabric of living came the golden thread of Tomanto and Teena and the bright thread of Miss Lottie.

It was late when they closed the book. Wilma smiled. Outside, the storm went on — the blinding, chilling rains; the raging wind. "It's like you said over the years, Nora. You always knew when a storm was coming for your pines whispered secrets..."

Nora finished for her. "Tomorrow the sun will shine. It always does, but first comes the wind." Her head went a little higher. Their eyes met. "I've been reading Isaiah again, Wilma, and I caught me another promise from God. It says, 'He stayed the rough wind in the day of the east wind.' "

Nora reached her trembling hand toward Wilma. Their gnarled fingers touched, interlocked. Outside the storm still rode its wild, frenzied course. But for Nora and Wilma, inside, deep inside, they were at peace.